The House Behind the Cedars

Charles W. Chesnutt

The House Behind the Cedars

Transaction Publishers

New Brunswick (U.S.A.) and London (U.K.)

145782

Copyright © 2000 by Transaction Publishers, New Brunswick, New Jersey.

All rights reserved under International and Pan-American Copyright Conventions. No part of this book may be reproduced or transmitted in any form or by any means, electronic or mechanical, including photocopy, recording, or any information storage and retrieval system, without prior permission in writing from the publisher. All inquiries should be addressed to Transaction Publishers, Rutgers—The State University, 35 Berrue Circle, Piscataway, NJ 08854–8042.

This book is printed on acid-free paper that meets the American National Standard for Permanence of Paper for Printed Library Materials.

Library of Congress Catalog Number: 99–30028
ISBN: 1–56000–494–0
Printed in the United States of America

Library of Congress Cataloging-in-Publication Data

Chesnutt, Charles Waddell, 1858–1932.
    The house behind the cedars / Charles W. Chesnutt.
      p. cm.
    ISBN 1–56000–494–0 (cloth : alk. paper)
    1. Afro-Americans—Southern States—Social conditions—Fiction.
2. Southern States—History—1865–1877—Fiction. 3. Racism—
Southern States—Fiction. 4. Mulattoes—Fiction. 5. Large type
books. I. Title.
[PS1292.C6H68   1999]
813'.4—dc21
                                                 99–30028
                                                    CIP

CONTENTS

THE HOUSE BEHIND THE CEDARS

I
A STRANGER FROM SOUTH CAROLINA

TIME touches all things with destroying hand; and if he seem now and then to bestow the bloom of youth, the sap of spring, it is but a brief mock cry, to be surely and swiftly followed by the wrinkles of old age, the dry leaves and bare branches of winter. And yet there are places where Time seems to linger lovingly long after youth has departed, and to which he seems loath to bring the evil day. Who has not known some even-tempered old man or woman who seemed to have drunk of the fountain of youth? Who has not seen somewhere an old town that, having long since ceased to grow, yet held its own without perceptible decline?

Some such trite reflection—as apposite to the subject as most random reflections are—passed through the mind of a young man who came out of the front door of the Patesville Hotel about nine o'clock one fine morning in spring, a few years after the Civil War, and started down Front Street toward the market-house. Arriving at the town late the previous evening, he had been driven up from the steamboat in a carriage, from which he had been able to distinguish only the shadowy outlines of the houses along the street; so that this morning walk was his first opportunity to see the town by daylight. He was dressed in a suit of linen duck—the day was warm—a panama straw hat, and patent leather shoes. In appearance he was tall, dark, with straight, black, lustrous hair, and very clean-cut, high-bred features. When he paused by the clerk's desk on his way out, to light his cigar, the day clerk, who had just come on duty, glanced at the register and read the last entry:—

"'John Warwick, Clarence, South Carolina.'

"One of the South Ca'lina bigbugs, I reckon—probably in cotton, or turpentine." The gentleman from South Carolina, walking down the street, glanced about him with an eager look, in which curiosity and affection were mingled with a touch of bitterness. He saw little that was not familiar, or that he had not seen in his dreams a hundred times during the past ten years. There had been some changes, it is true, some melancholy changes, but scarcely anything by way of addition or improvement to counterbalance them. Here and there blackened and dismantled walls marked the place where handsome buildings once had stood, for Sherman's march to the sea had left its mark upon the town. The stores were mostly of brick, two stories high, joining one another after the manner of cities. Some of the names on the signs were familiar; others, including a number of Jewish names, were quite unknown to him.

A two minutes' walk brought Warwick—the name he had registered under, and as we shall call him—to the market-house, the central feature of Patesville, from both the commercial and the picturesque points of view. Standing foursquare in the heart of the town, at the intersection of the two main streets, a "jog" at each street corner left around the market-house a little public square, which at this hour was well occupied by carts and wagons from the country and empty drays awaiting hire. Warwick was unable to perceive much change in the market-house. Perhaps the surface of the red brick, long unpainted, had scaled off a little more here and there. There might have been a slight accretion of the moss and lichen on the shingled roof. But the tall tower, with its four-faced clock, rose as majestically and uncompromisingly as though the land had never been subjugated. Was it so irreconcilable, Warwick wondered, as still to peal out the curfew bell, which at nine o'clock at night had clamorously warned all negroes, slave or free, that it was unlawful for them to be abroad after that hour, under penalty of imprisonment or whipping? Was the old constable, whose chief business it had been to ring the bell, still alive and exercising the functions of his office, and had age lessened or increased the number of times that obliging citizens performed this duty for him during his temporary absences in the company of convivial spirits? A few moments later, Warwick saw a colored policeman in the old constable's place—a stronger reminder than even the burned buildings that war had left its mark upon the old town, with which Time had dealt so tenderly.

The lower story of the market-house was open on all four of its sides to the public square. Warwick passed through one of the wide brick arches and traversed the building with a leisurely step. He looked in vain into the stalls for the butcher who had sold fresh meat twice a week, on market days, and he felt a genuine thrill of pleasure when he recognized the red bandana turban of old Aunt Lyddy, the ancient negro woman who had sold him gingerbread and fried fish, and told him weird tales of witchcraft and conjuration, in the old days when, as an idle boy, he had loafed about the market-house. He did not speak to her, however, or give her any sign of recognition. He threw a glance toward a certain corner where steps led to the town hall above. On this stairway he had once seen a manacled free negro shot while being taken upstairs for examination under a criminal charge. Warwick recalled vividly how the shot had rung out. He could see again the livid look of terror on the victim's face, the gathering crowd, the resulting confusion. The murderer, he recalled, had been tried and sentenced to imprisonment for life, but was pardoned by a merciful governor after serving a year of his sentence. As Warwick was neither a prophet nor the son of a prophet, he could not foresee that, thirty years later, even this would seem an excessive punishment for so slight a misdemeanor.

Leaving the market-house, Warwick turned to the left, and kept on his course until he reached the next corner. After another turn to the right, a dozen paces brought him in front of a small weather-beaten frame building, from which projected a wooden sign-board bearing the inscription:—

ARCHIBALD STRAIGHT,
LAWYER.

He turned the knob, but the door was locked. Retracing his steps past a vacant lot, the young man entered a shop where a colored man was employed in varnishing a coffin, which stood on two trestles in the middle of the floor. Not at all impressed by the melancholy suggestiveness of his task, he was whistling a lively air with great gusto.

Upon Warwick's entrance this effusion came to a sudden end, and the coffin-maker assumed an air of professional gravity.

"Good-mawnin', suh," he said, lifting his cap politely.

"Good-morning," answered Warwick. "Can you tell me anything about Judge Straight's office hours?"

"De ole jedge has be'n a little onreg'lar sence de wah, suh; but he gin'ally gits roun' 'bout ten o'clock er so. He's be'n kin' er feeble fer de las' few yeahs. An' I reckon," continued the undertaker solemnly, his glance unconsciously seeking a row of fine caskets standing against the wall,—"I reckon he'll soon be goin' de way er all de earth. 'Man dat is bawn er 'oman hath but a sho't time ter lib, an' is full er mis'ry. He cometh up an' is cut down lack as a flower.' 'De days er his life is three-sco' an' ten'— an' de ole jedge is libbed mo' d'n dat, suh, by five yeahs, ter say de leas'."

"'Death,'" quoted Warwick, with whose mood the undertaker's remarks were in tune, "'is the penalty that all must pay for the crime of living.'"

"Dat 's a fac', suh, dat 's a fac'; so dey mus'—so dey mus'. An' den all de dead has ter be buried. An' we does ou' sheer of it, suh, we does ou' sheer. We conduc's de obs'quies er all de bes' w'ite folks er de town, suh."

Warwick left the undertaker's shop and retraced his steps until he had passed the lawyer's office, toward which he threw an affectionate glance. A few rods farther led him past the old brick Presbyterian church, with its square tower, embowered in a stately grove; past the Catholic church, with its many crosses, and a painted wooden figure of St. James in a recess beneath the gable; and past the old Jefferson House, once the leading hotel of the town, in front of which political meetings had been held, and political speeches made, and political hard cider drunk, in the days of "Tippecanoe and Tyler too."

The street down which Warwick had come intersected Front Street at a sharp angle in front of the old hotel, forming a sort of flatiron block at the junction, known as Liberty Point,—perhaps because slave auctions were sometimes held there in the good old days. Just before Warwick reached Liberty Point, a young woman came down Front Street from the direction of the market-house. When their paths converged, Warwick kept on down Front Street behind her, it having been already his intention to walk in this direction.

Warwick's first glance had revealed the fact that the young woman was strikingly handsome, with a stately beauty seldom encountered. As he walked along behind her at a measured distance, he could not help noting the details that made up this pleasing impression, for his mind was singularly alive to beauty, in whatever embodiment. The girl's figure, he perceived, was admirably proportioned; she was evidently at the period when the angles of childhood were rounding into the promising curves of adolescence. Her abundant hair, of a dark and glossy brown, was neatly plaited and coiled above an ivory column that rose straight from a pair of gently sloping shoulders, clearly outlined beneath the light muslin frock that covered them. He could see that she was tastefully, though not richly, dressed, and that she walked with an elastic step that revealed a light heart and the vigor of perfect health. Her face, of course, he could not analyze, since he had caught only the one brief but convincing glimpse of it.

The young woman kept on down Front Street, Warwick maintaining his distance a few rods behind her. They passed a factory, a warehouse or two, and then, leaving the brick pavement, walked along on mother earth, under a leafy arcade of spreading oaks and elms. Their way led now through a residential portion of the town, which, as they advanced, gradually declined from staid respectability to poverty, open and unabashed. Warwick observed, as they passed through the respectable quarter, that few people who met the girl greeted her, and that some others whom she passed at gates or doorways gave her no sign of recognition; from which he inferred that she was possibly a visitor in the town and not well acquainted.

Their walk had continued not more than ten minutes when they crossed a creek by a wooden bridge and came to a row of mean houses standing flush with the street. At the door of one, an old black woman had stooped to lift a large basket, piled high with laundered clothes. The girl, as she passed, seized one end of the basket and helped the old woman to raise it to her head, where it rested solidly on the cushion of her head-kerchief. During this interlude, Warwick, though he had slackened his pace measurably, had so nearly closed the gap between himself and them as to hear the old woman say, with the dulcet negro intonation:—

"T'ank y', honey; de Lawd gwine bless you sho'. You wuz alluz a good gal, and de Lawd love eve'ybody w'at he'p de po' ole nigger. You gwine ter hab good luck all yo' bawn days."

"I hope you're a true prophet, Aunt Zilphy," laughed the girl in response.

The sound of her voice gave Warwick a thrill. It was soft and sweet and clear—quite in harmony with her appearance. That it had a faint suggestiveness of the old woman's accent he hardly noticed, for the current Southern speech, including his own, was rarely without a touch of it. The corruption of the white people's speech was one element—only one—of the negro's unconscious revenge for his own debasement.

The houses they passed now grew scattering, and the quarter of the town more neglected. Warwick felt himself wondering where the girl might be going in a neighborhood so uninviting. When she stopped to pull a half-naked negro child out of a mudhole and set him upon his feet, he thought she might be some young lady from the upper part of the town, bound on some errand of mercy, or going, perhaps, to visit an old servant or look for a new one. Once she threw a backward glance at Warwick, thus enabling him to catch a second glimpse of a singularly pretty face. Perhaps the young woman found his presence in the neighborhood as unaccountable as he had deemed hers; for, finding his glance fixed upon her, she quickened her pace with an air of startled timidity.

"A woman with such a figure," thought Warwick, "ought to be able to face the world with the confidence of Phryne confronting her judges."

By this time Warwick was conscious that something more than mere grace or beauty had attracted him with increasing force toward this young woman. A suggestion, at first faint and elusive, of something familiar, had grown stronger when he heard her voice, and became more and more pronounced with each rod of their advance; and when she stopped finally before a gate, and, opening it, went into a yard shut off from the street by a row of dwarf cedars, Warwick had already discounted in some measure the surprise he would have felt at seeing her enter there had he not walked down Front Street behind her. There was still sufficient unexpectedness about the act, however, to give him a decided thrill of pleasure.

"It must be Rena," he murmured. "Who could have dreamed that she would blossom out like that? It must surely be Rena!"

He walked slowly past the gate and peered through a narrow gap in the cedar hedge. The girl was moving along a sanded walk, toward a gray, unpainted house, with a steep roof, broken by dormer windows. The trace of timidity he had observed in her had given place to the more assured bearing of one who is upon his own ground. The garden walks were bordered by long rows of jonquils, pinks, and carnations, inclosing clumps of fragrant shrubs, lilies, and roses already in bloom. Toward the middle of the garden stood two fine magnolia-trees, with heavy, dark green, glistening leaves, while nearer the house two mighty elms shaded a wide piazza, at one end of which a honeysuckle vine, and at the other a Virginia creeper, running over a wooden lattice, furnished additional shade and seclusion. On dark or wintry days, the aspect of this garden must have been extremely sombre and depressing, and it might well have seemed a fit place to hide some guilty or disgraceful secret. But on the bright morning when Warwick stood looking through the cedars, it seemed, with its green frame and canopy and its bright carpet of flowers, an ideal retreat from the fierce sunshine and the sultry heat of the approaching summer.

The girl stooped to pluck a rose, and as she bent over it, her profile was clearly outlined. She held the flower to her face with a long-drawn inhalation, then went up the steps, crossed the piazza, opened the door without knocking, and entered the house with the air of one thoroughly at home.

"Yes," said the young man to himself, "it's Rena, sure enough."

The house stood on a corner, around which the cedar hedge turned, continuing along the side of the garden until it reached the line of the front of the house. The piazza to a rear wing, at right angles to the front of the house, was open to inspection from the side street, which, to judge from its deserted look, seemed to be but little used. Turning into this street and walking leisurely past the back yard, which was only slightly screened from the street by a china-tree, Warwick perceived the young woman standing on the piazza, facing an elderly woman, who sat in a large rocking-chair, plying a pair of knitting-needles on a half-finished stocking. Warwick's walk led him within three feet of the side gate, which he felt an almost irresistible impulse to enter. Every detail of the house and garden was familiar; a thousand cords of memory and affection drew him thither; but a stronger counter-motive prevailed. With a great effort he restrained himself, and after a momentary pause, walked slowly on past the house, with a backward glance, which he turned away when he saw that it was observed.

Warwick's attention had been so fully absorbed by the house behind the cedars and the women there, that he had scarcely noticed, on the other side of the neglected by-street, two men working by a large open window, in a low, rude building with a clapboarded roof, directly opposite the back piazza occupied by the two women. Both the men were busily engaged in shaping barrel-staves, each wielding a sharp-edged drawing-knife on a piece of seasoned oak clasped tightly in a wooden vise.

"I jes' wonder who dat man is, an' w'at he's doin' on dis street," observed the younger of the two, with a suspicious air. He had noticed the gentleman's involuntary pause and his interest in the opposite house, and had stopped work for a moment to watch the stranger as he went on down the street.

"Nev' min' 'bout dat man," said the elder one. "You 'ten' ter yo' wuk an' finish dat bairl-stave. You spen's enti'ely too much er yo' time stretchin' yo' neck atter other people. An' you need n' 'sturb yo'se'f 'bout dem folks 'cross de street, fer dey ain't yo' kin', an' you 're wastin' yo' time both'in' yo' min' wid 'em, er wid folks w'at comes on de street on account of 'em. Look sha'p now, boy, er you'll git dat stave trim' too much."

The younger man resumed his work, but still found time to throw a slanting glance out of the window. The gentleman, he perceived, stood for a moment on the rotting bridge across the old canal, and then walked slowly ahead until he turned to the right into Back Street, a few rods farther on.

II
AN EVENING VISIT

TOWARD evening of the same day, Warwick took his way down Front Street in the gathering dusk. By the time night had spread its mantle over the earth, he had reached the gate by which he had seen the girl of his morning walk enter the cedar-bordered garden. He stopped at the gate and glanced toward the house, which seemed dark and silent and deserted.

"It's more than likely," he thought, "that they are in the kitchen. I reckon I'd better try the back door."

But as he drew cautiously near the corner, he saw a man's figure outlined in the yellow light streaming from the open door of a small house between Front Street and the cooper shop. Wishing, for reasons of his own, to avoid observation, Warwick did not turn the corner, but walked on down Front Street until he reached a point from which he could see, at a long angle, a ray of light proceeding from the kitchen window of the house behind the cedars.

"They are there," he muttered with a sigh of relief, for he had feared they might be away. "I suspect I'll have to go to the front door, after all. No one can see me through the trees."

He retraced his steps to the front gate, which he essayed to open. There was apparently some defect in the latch, for it refused to work. Warwick remembered the trick, and with a slight sense of amusement, pushed his foot under the gate and gave it a hitch to the left, after which it opened readily enough. He walked softly up the sanded path, tiptoed up the steps and across the piazza, and rapped at the front door, not too loudly, lest this too might attract the attention of the man across the street. There was no response to his rap. He put his ear to the door and heard voices within, and the muffled sound of footsteps. After a moment he rapped again, a little louder than before.

There was an instant cessation of the sounds within. He rapped a third time, to satisfy any lingering doubt in the minds of those who he felt sure were listening in some trepidation. A moment later a ray of light streamed through the keyhole.

"Who's there?" a woman's voice inquired somewhat sharply.

"A gentleman," answered Warwick, not holding it yet time to reveal himself. "Does Mis' Molly Walden live here?"

"Yes," was the guarded answer. "I'm Mis' Walden. What's yo'r business?"

"I have a message to you from your son John."

A key clicked in the lock. The door opened, and the elder of the two women Warwick had seen upon the piazza stood in the doorway, peering curiously and with signs of great excitement into the face of the stranger.

"You've got a message from my son, you say?" she asked with tremulous agitation. "Is he sick, or in trouble?"

"No. He's well and doing well, and sends his love to you, and hopes you've not forgotten him."

"Fergot him? No, God knows I ain't fergot him! But come in, sir, an' tell me somethin' mo' about him."

Warwick went in, and as the woman closed the door after him, he threw a glance round the room. On the wall, over the mantelpiece, hung a steel engraving of

General Jackson at the battle of New Orleans, and, on the opposite wall, a framed fashion-plate from "Godey's Lady's Book." In the middle of the room an octagonal centre-table with a single leg, terminating in three sprawling feet, held a collection of curiously shaped sea-shells. There was a great haircloth sofa, somewhat the worse for wear, and a well-filled bookcase. The screen standing before the fireplace was covered with Confederate bank-notes of various denominations and designs, in which the heads of Jefferson Davis and other Confederate leaders were conspicuous.

> "Imperious Cæsar, dead, and turned to clay,
> Might stop a hole to keep the wind away,"

murmured the young man, as his eye fell upon this specimen of decorative art.

The woman showed her visitor to a seat. She then sat down facing him and looked at him closely. "When did you last see my son?" she asked.

"I've never met your son," he replied.

Her face fell. "Then the message comes through you from somebody else?"

"No, directly from your son."

She scanned his face with a puzzled look. This bearded young gentleman, who spoke so politely and was dressed so well, surely—no, it could not be! and yet—

Warwick was smiling at her through a mist of tears. An electric spark of sympathy flashed between them. They rose as if moved by one impulse, and were clasped in each other's arms.

"John, my John! It *is* John!"

"Mother—my dear old mother!"

14

"I did n't think," she sobbed, "that I'd ever see you again."

He smoothed her hair and kissed her. "And are you glad to see me, mother?"

"Am I glad to see you? It's like the dead comin' to life. I thought I'd lost you forever, John, my son, my darlin' boy!" she answered, hugging him strenuously.

"I could n't live without seeing you, mother," he said. He meant it, too, or thought he did, although he had not seen her for ten years.

"You've grown so tall, John, and are such a fine gentleman! And you *are* a gentleman now, John, ain't you— sure enough? Nobody knows the old story?"

"Well, mother, I've taken a man's chance in life, and have tried to make the most of it; and I haven't felt under any obligation to spoil it by raking up old stories that are best forgotten. There are the dear old books: have they been read since I went away?"

"No, honey, there's be'n nobody to read 'em, excep' Rena, an' she don't take to books quite like you did. But I've kep' 'em dusted clean, an' kep' the moths an' the bugs out; for I hoped you'd come back some day, an' knowed you'd like to find 'em all in their places, jus' like you left 'em."

"That's mighty nice of you, mother. You could have done no more if you had loved them for themselves. But where is Rena? I saw her on the street to-day, but she didn't know me from Adam; nor did I guess it was she until she opened the gate and came into the yard."

"I've be'n so glad to see you that I'd fergot about her," answered the mother. "Rena, oh, Rena!"

The girl was not far away; she had been standing in

the next room, listening intently to every word of the conversation, and only kept from coming in by a certain constraint that made a brother whom she had not met for so many years seem almost as much a stranger as if he had not been connected with her by any tie.

"Yes, mamma," she answered, coming forward.

"Rena, child, here 's yo'r brother John, who's come back to see us. Tell 'im howdy."

As she came forward, Warwick rose, put his arm around her waist, drew her toward him, and kissed her affectionately, to her evident embarrassment. She was a tall girl, but he towered above her in quite a protecting fashion; and she thought with a thrill how fine it would be to have such a brother as this in the town all the time. How proud she would be, if she could but walk up the street with such a brother by her side! She could then hold up her head before all the world, oblivious to the glance of pity or contempt. She felt a very pronounced respect for this tall gentleman who held her blushing face between his hands and looked steadily into her eyes.

"You 're the little sister I used to read stories to, and whom I promised to come and see some day. Do you remember how you cried when I went away?"

"It seems but yesterday," she answered. "I've still got the dime you gave me."

He kissed her again, and then drew her down beside him on the sofa, where he sat enthroned between the two loving and excited women. No king could have received more sincere or delighted homage. He was a man, come into a household of women,—a man of whom they were proud, and to whom they looked up with fond reverence. For he was not only a son,—a brother—but he represented to them the world from which circumstances had shut them out, and to which distance lent even more than its usual enchantment; and they felt nearer to this far-off world because of the glory which Warwick reflected from it.

"You're a very pretty girl," said Warwick, regarding his sister thoughtfully. "I followed you down Front Street this morning, and scarcely took my eyes off you all the way; and yet I did n't know you, and scarcely saw your face. You improve on acquaintance; to-night, I find you handsomer still."

"Now, John," said his mother, expostulating mildly, "you'll spile her, if you don't min'."

The girl was beaming with gratified vanity. What woman would not find such praise sweet from almost any source, and how much more so from this great man, who, from his exalted station in the world, must surely know the things whereof he spoke! She believed every word of it; she knew it very well indeed, but wished to hear it repeated and itemized and emphasized.

"No, he won't, mamma," she asserted, "for he 's flattering me. He talks as if I was some rich young lady, who lives on the Hill,"—the Hill was the aristocratic portion of the town,—"instead of a poor"—

"Instead of a poor young girl, who has the hill to climb," replied her brother, smoothing her hair with his hand. Her hair was long and smooth and glossy, with a wave like the ripple of a summer breeze upon the surface of still water. It was the girl's great pride, and had been sedulously cared for. "What lovely hair! It has just the wave that yours lacks, mother."

"Yes," was the regretful reply, "I've never be'n able to

git that wave out. But her hair 's be 'n took good care of, an' there ain't nary gal in town that's got any finer."

"Don't worry about the wave, mother. It's just the fashionable ripple, and becomes her immensely. I think my little Albert favors his Aunt Rena somewhat."

"Your little Albert!" they cried. "You've got a child?"

"Oh, yes," he replied calmly, "a very fine baby boy."

They began to purr in proud contentment at this information, and made minute inquiries about the age and weight and eyes and nose and other important details of this precious infant. They inquired more coldly about the child's mother, of whom they spoke with greater warmth when they learned that she was dead. They hung breathless on Warwick's words as he related briefly the story of his life since he had left, years before, the house behind the cedars—how with a stout heart and an abounding hope he had gone out into a seemingly hostile world, and made fortune stand and deliver. His story had for the women the charm of an escape from captivity, with all the thrill of a pirate's tale. With the whole world before him, he had remained in the South, the land of his fathers, where, he conceived, he had an inalienable birthright. By some good chance he had escaped military service in the Confederate army, and, in default of older and more experienced men, had undertaken, during the rebellion, the management of a large estate, which had been left in the hands of women and slaves. He had filled the place so acceptably, and employed his leisure to such advantage, that at the close of the war he found himself— he was modest enough to think, too, in default of a better man—the husband of the orphan daughter of the gentleman who had owned the plantation, and who had

18

lost his life upon the battlefield. Warwick's wife was of good family, and in a more settled condition of society it would not have been easy for a young man of no visible antecedents to win her hand. A year or two later, he had taken the oath of allegiance, and had been admitted to the South Carolina bar. Rich in his wife's right, he had been able to practice his profession upon a high plane, without the worry of sordid cares, and with marked success for one of his age.

"I suppose," he concluded, "that I have got along at the bar, as elsewhere, owing to the lack of better men. Many of the good lawyers were killed in the war, and most of the remainder were disqualified; while I had the advantage of being alive, and of never having been in arms against the government. People had to have lawyers, and they gave me their business in preference to the carpet-baggers. Fortune, you know, favors the available man."

His mother drank in with parted lips and glistening eyes the story of his adventures and the record of his successes. As Rena listened, the narrow walls that hemmed her in seemed to draw closer and closer, as though they must crush her. Her brother watched her keenly. He had been talking not only to inform the women, but with a deeper purpose, conceived since his morning walk, and deepened as he had followed, during his narrative, the changing expression of Rena's face and noted her intense interest in his story, her pride in his successes, and the occasional wistful look that indexed her self-pity so completely.

"An' I s'pose you're happy, John?" asked his mother.

"Well, mother, happiness is a relative term, and depends, I imagine, upon how nearly we think we get what we think we want. I have had my chance and haven't thrown it away, and I suppose I ought to be happy. But then, I have lost my wife, whom I loved very dearly, and who loved me just as much, and I'm troubled about my child."

"Why?" they demanded. "Is there anything the matter with him?"

"No, not exactly. He's well enough, as babies go, and has a good enough nurse, as nurses go. But the nurse is ignorant, and not always careful. A child needs some woman of its own blood to love it and look after it intelligently."

Mis' Molly's eyes were filled with tearful yearning. She would have given all the world to warm her son's child upon her bosom; but she knew this could not be.

"Did your wife leave any kin?" she asked with an effort.

"No near kin; she was an only child."

"You'll be gettin' married again," suggested his mother.

"No," he replied; "I think not."

Warwick was still reading his sister's face, and saw the spark of hope that gleamed in her expressive eye.

"If I had some relation of my own that I could take into the house with me," he said reflectively, "the child might be healthier and happier, and I should be much more at ease about him."

The mother looked from son to daughter with a dawning apprehension and a sudden pallor. When she saw the yearning in Rena's eyes, she threw herself at her son's feet.

"Oh, John," she cried despairingly, "don't take her

away from me! Don't take her, John, darlin', for it'd break my heart to lose her!"

Rena's arms were round her mother's neck, and Rena's voice was sounding in her ears. "There, there, mamma! Never mind! I won't leave you, mamma—dear old mamma! Your Rena'll stay with you always, and never, never leave you."

John smoothed his mother's hair with a comforting touch, patted her withered cheek soothingly, lifted her tenderly to her place by his side, and put his arm about her.

"You love your children, mother?"

They're all I've got," she sobbed, "an' they cos' me all I had. When the las' one's gone, I'll want to go too, for I'll be all alone in the world. Don't take Rena, John; for if you do, I'll never see her again, an' I can't bear to think of it. How would you like to lose yo'r one child?"

"Well, well, mother, we'll say no more about it. And now tell me all about yourself, and about the neighbors, and how you got through the war, and who's dead and who's married—and everything."

The change of subject restored in some degree Mis' Molly's equanimity, and with returning calmness came a sense of other responsibilities.

"Good gracious, Rena!" she exclaimed. John 's be'n in the house an hour, and ain't had nothin' to eat yet! Go in the kitchen an' spread a clean tablecloth, an' git out that 'tater pone, an' a pitcher o' that las' kag o' persimmon beer, an' let John take a bite an' a sip."

Warwick smiled at the mention of these homely dainties. "I thought of your sweet-potato pone at the hotel to-day, when I was at dinner, and wondered if you'd have some in the house. There was never any like yours; and I've forgotten the taste of persimmon beer entirely."

Rena left the room to carry out her hospitable commission. Warwick, taking advantage of her absence, returned after a while to the former subject.

"Of course, mother," he said calmly, "I wouldn't think of taking Rena away against your wishes. A mother's claim upon her child is a high and holy one. Of course she will have no chance here, where our story is known. The war has wrought great changes, has put the bottom rail on top, and all that—but it has n't wiped *that* out. Nothing but death can remove that stain, if it does not follow us even beyond the grave. Here she must forever be—nobody! With me she might have got out into the world; with her beauty she might have made a good marriage; and, if I mistake not, she has sense as well as beauty."

"Yes," sighed the mother, "she 's got good sense. She ain't as quick as you was, an' don't read as many books, but she 's keerful an' painstakin', an' always tries to do what 's right. She 's be'n thinkin' about goin' away somewhere an' tryin' to git a school to teach, er somethin', sence the Yankees have started 'em everywhere for po' white folks an' niggers, too. But I don't like fer her to go too fur."

"With such beauty and brains," continued Warwick, "she could leave this town and make a place for herself. The place is already made. She has only to step into my carriage—after perhaps a little preparation—and ride up the hill which I have had to climb so painfully. It would be a great pleasure to me to see her at the top. But of course it is impossible—a mere idle dream. *Your* claim comes first; her duty chains her here."

"It would be so lonely without her," murmured the mother weakly, "an' I love her so—my las' one!"

"No doubt—no doubt," returned Warwick, with a sympathetic sigh; "of course you love her. It 's not to be thought of for a moment. It 's a pity that she could n't have a chance here—but how could she? I had thought she might marry a gentleman; but I dare say she 'll do as well as the rest of her friends—as well as Mary B., for instance, who married—Homer Pettifoot, did you say? Or maybe Billy Oxendine might do for her. As long as she has never known an better, she 'll probably be as well satisfied as though she married a rich man, and lived in a fine house, and kept a carriage and servants, and moved with the best in the land."

The tortured mother could endure no more. The one thing she desired above all others was her daughter's happiness. Her own life had not been governed by the highest standards, but about her love for her beautiful daughter there was no taint of selfishness. The life her son had described had been to her always the ideal but unattainable life. Circumstances, some beyond her control, and others for which she was herself in a measure responsible, had put it forever and inconceivably beyond her reach. It had been conquered by her son. It beckoned to her daughter. The comparison of this free and noble life with the sordid existence of those around her broke down the last barrier of opposition.

"O Lord!" she moaned, "what shall I do without her? It 'll be lonely, John—so lonely!"

"You 'll have your home, mother," said Warwick tenderly, accepting the implied surrender. "You 'll have your friends and relatives, and the knowledge that your children are happy. I'll let you hear from us often, and no doubt you can see Rena now and then. But you must let her go, mother,—it would be a sin against her to refuse."

"She may go," replied the mother brokenly. "I'll not stand in her way—I've got sins enough to answer for already."

Warwick watched her pityingly. He had stirred her feelings to unwonted depths, and his sympathy went out to her. If she had sinned, she had been more sinned against than sinning, and it was not his part to judge her. He had yielded to a sentimental weakness in deciding upon this trip to Patesville. A matter of business had brought him within a day's journey of the town, and an overmastering impulse had compelled him to seek the mother who had given him birth and the old town where he had spent the earlier years of his life. No one would have acknowledged sooner than he the folly of this visit. Men who have elected to govern their lives by principles of abstract right and reason, which happen, perhaps, to be at variance with what society considers equally right and reasonable, should, for fear of complications, be careful about descending from the lofty heights of logic to the common level of impulse and affection. Many years before, Warwick, when a lad of eighteen, had shaken the dust of the town from his feet, and with it, he fondly thought, the blight of his inheritance, and had achieved elsewhere a worthy career. But during all these years of absence he had cherished a tender feeling for his mother, and now again found himself in her house, amid the familiar surroundings of his childhood. His visit had brought joy to his mother's heart, and was now to bring its shrouded companion, sorrow. His mother had lived her life, for good or ill. A wider door was open to his sister—her mother must not bar the entrance.

"She may go," the mother repeated sadly, drying her tears. "I 'll give her up for her good."

"The table 's ready, mamma," said Rena, coming to the door.

The lunch was spread in the kitchen, a large unplastered room at the rear, with a wide fireplace at one end. Only yesterday, it seemed to Warwick, he had sprawled upon the hearth, turning sweet potatoes before the fire, or roasting groundpeas in the ashes; or, more often, reading, by the light of a blazing pine-knot or lump of resin, some volume from the bookcase in the hall. From Bulwer's novel, he had read the story of Warwick the Kingmaker, and upon leaving home had chosen it for his own. He was a new man, but he had the blood of an old race, and he would select for his own one of its worthy names. Overhead loomed the same smoky beams, decorated with what might have been, from all appearances, the same bunches of dried herbs, the same strings of onions and red peppers. Over in the same corner stood the same spinning-wheel, and through the open door of an adjoining room he saw the old loom, where in childhood he had more than once thrown the shuttle. The kitchen was different from the stately dining-room of the old colonial mansion where he now lived; but it was homelike, and it was familiar. The sight of it moved his heart, and he felt for the moment a sort of a blind anger against the fate which made it necessary that he should visit the home of his childhood, if at all, like a thief in the night. But he realized, after a moment, that the thought was pure sentiment, and that one who had gained so much ought not to complain if he must give up a little. He who would climb the heights of life must leave even the pleasantest valleys behind.

"Rena," asked her mother, "how 'd you like to go an' pay yo'r brother John a visit? I guess I might spare you for a little while."

The girl's eyes lighted up. She would not have gone if her mother had wished her to stay, but she would always have regarded this as the lost opportunity of her life.

"Are you sure you don't care, mamma?" she asked, hoping and yet doubting.

"Oh, I 'll manage to git along somehow or other. You can go an' stay till you git homesick, an' then John 'll let you come back home."

But Mis' Molly believed that she would never come back, except, like her brother, under cover of the night. She must lose her daughter as well as her son, and this should be the penance for her sin. That her children must expiate as well the sins of their fathers, who had sinned so lightly, after the manner of men, neither she nor they could foresee, since they could not read the future.

The next boat by which Warwick could take his sister away left early in the morning of the next day but one. He went back to his hotel with the understanding that the morrow should be devoted to getting Rena ready for her departure, and that Warwick would visit the household again the following evening; for, as has been intimated, there were several reasons why there should be no open relations between the fine gentleman at the hotel and the women in the house behind the cedars, who, while superior in blood and breeding to the people of

26

the neighborhood in which they lived, were yet under the shadow of some cloud which clearly shut them out from the better society of the town. Almost any resident could have given one or more of these reasons, of which any one would have been sufficient to most of them; and to some of them Warwick's mere presence in the town would have seemed a bold and daring thing.

III
THE OLD JUDGE

ON the morning following the visit to his mother, Warwick visited the old judge's office. The judge was not in, but the door stood open, and Warwick entered to await his return. There had been fewer changes in the office, where he had spent many, many hours, than in the town itself. The dust was a little thicker, the papers in the pigeon-holes of the walnut desk were a little yellower, the cobwebs in the corners a little more aggressive. The flies droned as drowsily and the murmur of the brook below was just as audible. Warwick stood at the rear window and looked out over a familiar view. Directly across the creek, on the low ground beyond, might be seen the dilapidate stone foundation of the house where once had lived Flora Macdonald, the Jacobite refugee, the most romantic character of North Carolina history. Old Judge Straight had had a tree cut away from the creek-side opposite his window, so that this historic ruin might be visible from his office; for the judge could trace the ties of blood that connected him collaterally with this famous personage. His pamphlet on Flora Macdonald, printed for private circulation, was highly prized by those of his friends who were fortunate enough to obtain a copy. To the left of the window a placid mill-pond spread its wide expanse, and to the right the creek disappeared under a canopy of overhanging trees.

A footstep sounded in the doorway, and Warwick, turning, faced the old judge. Time had left greater marks upon the lawyer than upon his office. His hair was whiter, his stoop more pronounced; when he spoke to Warwick, his voice had some of the shrillness of old age; and in his hand, upon which the veins stood out prominently, a decided tremor was perceptible.

"Good-morning, Judge Straight," said the young man, removing his hat with the graceful Southern deference of the young for the old.

Good-morning, sir," replied the judge with equal courtesy.

"You don't remember me, I imagine," suggested Warwick.

"Your face seems familiar," returned the judge cautiously, "but I cannot for the moment recall your name. I shall be glad to have you refresh my memory."

"I was John Walden, sir, when you knew me."

The judge's face still gave no answering light of recognition.

"Your old office-boy," continued the younger man.

"Ah, indeed, so you were!" rejoined the judge warmly, extending his hand with great cordiality, and inspecting Warwick more closely through his spectacles. "Let me see— you went away a few years before the war, was n't it?"

"Yes, sir, to South Carolina."

"Yes, yes, I remember now! I had been thinking it was to the North. So many things have happened since then, that it taxes an old man's memory to keep track of them all. Well, well! and how have you been getting along?"

Warwick told his story in outline, much as he had given it to his mother and sister, and the judge seemed very much interested.

"And you married into a good family?" he asked.

"Yes, sir."

"And have children?"

"One."

"And you are visiting your mother?"

"Not exactly. I have seen her, but I am stopping at a hotel."

"H'm! Are you staying long?"

"I leave to-morrow."

"It's well enough. I would n't stay too long. The people of a small town are inquisitive about strangers, and some of them have long memories. I remember we went over the law, which was in your favor; but custom is stronger than law—in these matters custom *is* law. It was a great pity that your father did not make a will. Well, my boy, I wish you continued good luck; I imagined you would make your way."

Warwick went away, and the old judge sat for a moment absorbed in reflection. "Right and wrong," he mused, "must be eternal verities, but our standards for measuring them vary with our latitude and our epoch. We make our customs lightly; once made, like our sins, they grip us in bands of steel; we become the creatures of our creations. By one standard my old office-boy should never have been born. Yet he is a son of Adam, and came into existence in the way ordained by God from the beginning of the world. In equity he would seem to be entitled to his chance in life; it might have been wiser, though, for him to seek it farther afield than South Carolina. It was too near home, even though the laws were with him."

IV
DOWN THE RIVER

NEITHER mother nor daughter slept a great deal during the night of Warwick's first visit. Mis' Molly anointed her sacrifice with tears and cried herself to sleep. Rena's emotions were more conflicting; she was sorry to leave her mother, but glad to go with her brother. The mere journey she was about to make was a great event for the two women to contemplate, to say nothing of the golden vision that lay beyond, for neither of them had ever been out of the town or its vicinity.

The next day was devoted to preparations for the journey. Rena's slender wardrobe was made ready and packed in a large valise. Towards sunset, Mis' Molly took off her apron, put on her slat-bonnet,—she was ever the pink of neatness,—picked her way across the street, which was muddy from a rain during the day, traversed the foot-bridge that spanned the ditch in front of the cooper shop, and spoke first to the elder of the two men working there.

"Good-evenin', Peter."

"Good-evenin', ma'm," responded the man briefly, and not relaxing at all the energy with which he was trimming a barrel-stave.

Mis' Molly then accosted the younger workman, a dark-brown young man, small in stature, but with a well-shaped head, an expressive forehead, and features indicative of kindness, intelligence, humor, and imagination. "Frank," she asked, "can I git you to do somethin' fer me soon in the mo'nin'?"

"Yas'm, I reckon so," replied the young man, resting his hatchet on the chopping-block. "W'at is it, Mis' Molly?"

"My daughter 'goin' away on the boat, an' I 'lowed you would n' min' totin' her kyarpet-bag down to the w'arf, onless you'd ruther haul it down on yo'r kyart. It ain't very heavy. Of co'se I'll pay you fer yo'r trouble."

"Thank y', ma'm," he replied. He knew that she would not pay him, for the simple reason that he would not accept pay for such a service. "Is she gwine fur?" he asked, with a sorrowful look, which he could not entirely disguise.

"As fur as Wilmin'ton an' beyon'. She'll be visitin' her brother John, who lives in—another State, an' wants her to come an' see him."

"Yas 'm, I'll come. I won' need de kyart—I'll tote de bag. 'Bout w'at time shill I come over?"

"Well, 'long 'bout seven o'clock or half pas'. She's goin' on the Old North State, an' it leaves at eight."

Frank stood looking after Mis' Molly as she picked her way across the street, until he was recalled to his duty by a sharp word from his father.

31

"'Ten' ter yo' wuk, boy, 'ten' ter yo' wuk. You 're wastin' yo' time—wastin' yo' time!"

Yes, he was wasting his time. The beautiful young girl across the street could never be anything to him. But he had saved her life once, and had dreamed that he might render her again some signal service that might win her friendship, and convince her of his humble devotion. For Frank was not proud. A smile, which Peter would have regarded as condescending to a free man, who, since the war, was as good as anybody else; a kind word, which Peter would have considered offensively patronizing; a piece of Mis' Molly's famous potato pone from Rena's hands,—a bone to a dog, Peter called it once;—were ample rewards for the thousand and one small services Frank had rendered the two women who lived in the house behind the cedars.

Frank went over in the morning a little ahead of the appointed time, and waited on the back piazza until his services were required.

"You ain't gwine ter be gone long, is you, Miss Rena?" he inquired, when Rena came out dressed for the journey in her best frock, with broad white collar and cuffs.

Rena did not know. She had been asking herself the same question. All sorts of vague dreams had floated through her mind during the last few hours, as to what the future might bring forth. But she detected the anxious note in Frank's voice, and had no wish to give this faithful friend of the family unnecessary pain.

"Oh, no, Frank, I reckon not. I'm supposed to be just going on a short visit. My brother has lost his wife, and wishes me to come and stay with him awhile, and look after his little boy."

"I'm feared you'll lack it better dere, Miss Rena," replied Frank sorrowfully, dropping his mask of unconcern, "an' den you won't come back, an' none er yo' frien's won't never see you no mo'."

"You don't think, Frank," asked Rena severely, "that I would leave my mother and my home and all my friends, and *never* come back again?"

"Why, no 'ndeed," interposed Mis' Molly wistfully, as she hovered around her daughter, giving her hair or her gown a touch here and there; "she 'll be so homesick in a month that she'll be willin' to walk home."

"You would n' never hafter do dat, Miss Rena," returned Frank, with a disconsolate smile. "Ef you ever wanter come home, an' can't git back no other way, jes' let *me* know, an' I'll take my mule an' my kyart an' fetch you back, ef it 's from de een' er de worl'."

"Thank you, Frank, I believe you would," said the girl kindly. "You're a true friend, Frank, and I'll not forget you while I'm gone."

The idea of her beautiful daughter riding home from the end of the world with Frank, in a cart, behind a one-eyed mule, struck Mis' Molly as the height of the ridiculous—she was in a state of excitement where tears or laughter would have come with equal ease—and she turned away to hide her merriment. Her daughter was going to live in a fine house, and marry a rich man, and ride in her carriage. Of course a negro would drive the carriage, but that was different from riding with one in a cart.

When it was time to go, Mis' Molly and Rena set out on foot for the river, which was only a short distance away. Frank followed with the valise. There was no gathering of friends to see Rena off, as might have been the case under different circumstances. Her departure had some of the characteristics of a secret flight; it was as important that her destination should not be known, as it had been that her brother should conceal his presence in the town.

Mis' Molly and Rena remained on the bank until the steamer announced, with a raucous whistle, its readiness to depart. Warwick was seen for a moment on the upper deck, from which he greeted them with a smile and a slight nod. He had bidden his mother an affectionate farewell the evening before. Rena gave her hand to Frank.

"Good-by, Frank," she said, with a kind smile; "I hope you and mamma will be good friends while I'm gone."

The whistle blew a second warning blast, and the deck hands prepared to draw in the gang-plank. Rena flew into her mother's arms, and then, breaking away, hurried on board and retired to her state-room, from which she did not emerge during the journey. The window-blinds were closed, darkening the room, and the stewardess who came to ask if she should bring her some dinner could not see her face distinctly, but perceived enough to make her surmise that the young lady had been weeping.

"Po' chile," murmured the sympathetic colored woman, "I reckon some er her folks is dead, er her sweetheart 's gone back on her, er e'se she 's had some kin'er bad luck er 'nuther. W'ite folks has deir troubles jes' ez well ez black folks, an' sometimes feels 'em mo', 'cause dey ain't ez use' ter 'em."

Mis' Molly went back in sadness to the lonely house behind the cedars, henceforth to be peopled for her with

34

only the memory of those she had loved. She had paid with her heart's blood another installment on the Shylock's bond exacted by society for her own happiness of the past and her children's prospects for the future.

The journey down the sluggish river to the sea-board in the flat-bottomed, stern-wheel steamer lasted all day and most of the night. During the first half-day, the boat grounded now and then upon a sand-bank, and the half-naked negro deck-hands toiled with ropes and poles to release it. Several times before Rena fell asleep that night, the steamer would tie up at a landing, and by the light of huge pine torches she watched the boat hands send the yellow turpentine barrels down the steep bank in a long string, or pass cord-wood on board from hand to hand. The excited negroes, their white teeth and eye-balls glistening in the surrounding darkness to which their faces formed no relief ; the white officers in brown linen, shouting, swearing, and gesticulating; the yellow, flickering torchlight over all,—made up a scene of which the weird interest would have appealed to a more *blasé* traveler than this girl upon her first journey.

During the day, Warwick had taken his meals in the dining-room, with the captain and the other cabin passengers. It was learned that he was a South Carolina lawyer, and not a carpet-bagger. Such credentials were unimpeachable, and the passengers found him a very agreeable traveling companion. Apparently sound on the subject of negroes, Yankees, and the righteousness of the lost cause, he yet discussed these themes in a lofty and impersonal manner that gave his words greater weight than if he had seemed warped by a personal grievance. His attitude, in fact, piqued the curiosity of one or two of the passengers.

"Did your people lose any niggers?" asked one of them.

"My father owned a hundred," he replied grandly.

Their respect for his views was doubled. It is easy to moralize about the misfortunes of others, and to find good in the evil that they suffer;—only a true philosopher could speak thus lightly of his own losses.

When the steamer tied up at the wharf at Wilmington, in the early morning, the young lawyer and a veiled lady passenger drove in the same carriage to a hotel. After they had breakfasted in a private room, Warwick explained to his sister the plan he had formed for her future. Henceforth she must be known as Miss Warwick, dropping the old name with the old life. He would place her for a year in a boarding-school at Charleston, after which she would take her place as the mistress of his house. Having imparted this information, he took his sister for a drive through the town. There for the first time Rena saw great ships, which, her brother told her, sailed across the mighty ocean to distant lands, whose flags he pointed out drooping lazily at the mast-heads. The business portion of the town had "an ancient and fishlike smell," and most of the trade seemed to be in cotton and naval stores and products of the sea. The wharves were piled high with cotton bales, and there were acres of barrels of resin and pitch and tar and spirits of turpentine. The market, a long, low, wooden structure, in the middle of the principal street, was filled with a mass of people of all shades, from blue-black to Saxon blonde, gabbling and gesticulating over piles of oysters and clams and freshly caught fish of varied hue. By ten o'clock the sun was beating down so fiercely that the glitter of the white, sandy streets dazzled and pained the eyes unaccustomed to it, and Rena was glad to be driven back to the hotel. The travelers left together on an early afternoon train.

Thus for the time being was severed the last tie that bound Rena to her narrow past, and for some time to come the places and the people who had known her once were to know her no more.

Some few weeks later, Mis' Molly called upon old Judge Straight with reference to the taxes on her property.

"Your son came in to see me the other day," he remarked. "He seems to have got along."

"Oh, yes, judge, he's done fine, John has; an' he 's took his sister away with him."

"Ah!" exclaimed the judge. Then after a pause he added, "I hope she may do as well."

"Thank you, sir," she said, with a curtsy, as she rose to go. "We've always knowed that you were our friend and wished us well."

The judge looked after her as she walked away. Her bearing had a touch of timidity, a shade of affectation, and yet a certain pathetic dignity.

"It is a pity," he murmured, with a sigh, "that men cannot select their mothers. My young friend John has builded, whether wisely or not, very well; but he has come back into the old life and carried away a part of it, and I fear that this addition will weaken the structure."

V
THE TOURNAMENT

THE annual tournament of the Clarence Social Club was about to begin. The county fairground, where all was in readiness, sparkled with the youth and beauty of the town, standing here and there under the trees in animated groups, or moving toward the seats from which the pageant might be witnessed. A quarter of a mile of the race track, to right and left of the judges' stand, had been laid off for the lists. Opposite the grand stand, which occupied a considerable part of this distance, a dozen uprights had been erected at measured intervals. Projecting several feet over the track from each of these uprights was an iron crossbar, from which an iron hook depended. Between the uprights stout posts were planted, of such a height that their tops could be easily reached by a swinging sword-cut from a mounted rider passing upon the track. The influence of Walter Scott was strong upon the old South. The South before the war was essentially feudal, and Scott's novels of chivalry appealed forcefully to the feudal heart. During the month preceding the Clarence tournament, the local bookseller had closed out his entire stock of "Ivanhoe," consisting of five copies, and had taken orders for seven copies more. The tournament scene in this popular novel furnished the model after which these bloodless imitations of the ancient passages-at-arms were conducted, with such variations as were required to adapt them to a different age and civilization.

The best people gradually filled the grand stand, while the poorer white and colored folks found seats outside, upon what would now be known as the "bleachers," or stood alongside the lists. The knights, masquerading in fanciful costumes, in which bright-colored garments, gilt paper, and cardboard took the place of knightly harness, were mounted on spirited horses. Most of them were gathered at one end of the lists, while others practiced their steeds upon the unoccupied portion of the race track.

The judges entered the grand stand, and one of them, after looking at his watch, gave a signal. Immediately a herald, wearing a bright yellow sash, blew a loud blast upon a bugle, and, big with the importance of his office, galloped wildly down the lists. An attendant on horseback busied himself hanging upon each of the pendent hooks an iron ring, of some two inches in diameter, while another, on foot, placed on top of each of the shorter posts a wooden ball some four inches through.

"It's my first tournament," observed a lady near the front of the grand stand, leaning over and addressing John Warwick, who was seated in the second row, in company with a very handsome girl. "It is somewhat different from Ashby-de-la-Zouch."

"It is the renaissance of chivalry, Mrs. Newberry," replied the young lawyer, "and, like any other renaissance, it must adapt itself to new times and circumstances. For instance, when we build a Greek portico, having no Pentelic marble near at hand, we use a pine-tree, one of nature's columns, which Grecian art at its best could only copy and idealize. Our knights are not weighted down with heavy armor, but much more appropriately attired, for a day like this, in costumes that recall the picturesqueness, without the discomfort, of the old knightly harness.

For an iron-headed lance we use a wooden substitute, with which we transfix rings instead of hearts; while our trusty blades hew their way through wooden blocks instead of through flesh and blood. It is a South Carolina renaissance which has points of advantage over the tournaments of the olden time."

"I'm afraid, Mr. Warwick," said the lady, "that you 're the least bit heretical about our chivalry—or else you 're a little too deep for me."

"The last would be impossible, Mrs. Newberry; and I'm sure our chivalry has proved its valor on many a hard-fought field. The spirit of a thing, after all, is what counts; and what is lacking here? We have the lists, the knights, the prancing steeds, the trial of strength and skill. If our knights do not run the physical risks of Ashby-de-la-Zouch, they have all the mental stimulus. Wounded vanity will take the place of wounded limbs, and there will be broken hopes in lieu of broken heads. How many hearts in yonder group of gallant horsemen beat high with hope! How many possible Queens of Love and Beauty are in this group of fair faces that surround us!"

The lady was about to reply, when the bugle sounded again, and the herald dashed swiftly back upon his prancing steed to the waiting group of riders. The horsemen formed three abreast, and rode down the lists in orderly array. As they passed the grand stand, each was conscious of the battery of bright eyes turned upon him, and each gave by his bearing some idea of his ability to stand fire from such weapons. One horse pranced proudly, another caracoled with grace. One rider fidgeted nervously, another trembled and looked the other way. Each horseman carried in his hand a long wooden lance and wore at his side a cavalry sabre, of which there were plenty to be had since the war, at small expense. Several left the ranks and drew up momentarily beside the grand stand, where they took from fair hands a glove or a flower, which was pinned upon the rider's breast or fastened upon his hat—a ribbon or a veil, which was tied about the lance like a pennon, but far enough from the point not to interfere with the usefulness of the weapon.

As the troop passed the lower end of the grand stand, a horse, excited by the crowd, became somewhat unmanageable, and in the effort to curb him, the rider dropped his lance. The prancing animal reared, brought one of his hoofs down upon the fallen lance with considerable force, and sent a broken piece of it flying over the railing opposite the grand stand, into the middle of a group of spectators standing there. The flying fragment was dodged by those who saw it coming, but brought up with a resounding thwack against the head of a colored man in the second row, who stood watching the grand stand with an eager and curious gaze. He rubbed his head ruefully, and made a good-natured response to the chaffing of his neighbors, who, seeing no great harm done, made witty and original remarks about the advantage of being black upon occasions where one's skull was exposed to danger. Finding that the blow had drawn blood, the young man took out a red bandana handkerchief and tied it around his head, meantime letting his eye roam over the faces in the grand stand, as though in search of some one that he expected or hoped to find there.

The knights, having reached the end of the lists, now turned and rode back in open order, with such skillful horsemanship as to evoke a storm of applause from the spectators. The ladies in the grand stand waved their handkerchiefs vigorously, and the men clapped their hands. The beautiful girl seated by Warwick's side accidentally let a little square of white lace-trimmed linen slip from her hand. It fluttered lightly over the railing, and, buoyed up by the air, settled slowly toward the lists. A young rider in the approaching rear rank saw the handkerchief fall, and darting swiftly forward, caught it on the point of his lance ere it touched the ground. He drew up his horse and made a movement as though to extend the handkerchief toward the lady, who was blushing profusely at the attention she had attracted by her carelessness. The rider hesitated a moment, glanced interrogatively at Warwick, and receiving a smile in return, tied the handkerchief around the middle of his lance and quickly rejoined his comrades at the head of the lists.

The young man with the bandage round his head, on the benches across the lists, had forced his way to the front row and was leaning against the railing. His restless eye was attracted by the falling handkerchief, and his face, hitherto anxious, suddenly lit up with animation.

"Yas, suh, yas, suh, it's her!" he muttered softly. "It's Miss Rena, sho 's you bawn. She looked lack a' angel befo', but now, up dere 'mongs' all dem rich, fine folks, she looks lack a whole flock er angels. Dey ain' one er dem ladies w'at could hol' a candle ter her. I wonder w'at dat man's gwine ter do wid her handkercher? I s'pose he 's her gent'eman now. I wonder ef she'd know me er speak ter me ef she seed me? I reckon she would, spite er her gittin' up so in de worl'; fer she wuz alluz good ter ev'ybody, an' dat let even *me* in," he concluded with a sigh.

"Who is the lady, Tryon?" asked one of the young men, addressing the knight who had taken the handkerchief.

"A Miss Warwick," replied the knight pleasantly, "Miss Rowena Warwick, the lawyer's sister."

"I did n't know he had a sister," rejoined the first speaker. "I envy you your lady. There are six Rebeccas and eight Rowenas of my own acquaintance in the grand stand, but she throws them all into the shade. She hasn't been here long, surely; I haven't seen her before."

"She has been away at school; she came only last night," returned the knight of the crimson sash, briefly. He was already beginning to feel a proprietary interest in the lady whose token he wore, and did not care to discuss her with a casual acquaintance.

The herald sounded the charge. A rider darted out from the group and galloped over the course. As he passed under each ring, he tried to catch it on the point of his lance,—a feat which made the management of the horse with the left hand necessary, and required a true eye and a steady arm. The rider captured three of the twelve rings, knocked three others off the hooks, and left six undisturbed. Turning at the end of the lists, he took the lance with the reins in the left hand and drew his sword with the right. He then rode back over the course, cutting at the wooden balls upon the posts. Of these he clove one in twain, to use the parlance of chivalry, and knocked two others off their supports. His performance was greeted with a liberal measure of applause, for which he bowed in smiling acknowledgment as he took his place among the riders.

Again the herald's call sounded, and the tourney went forward. Rider after rider, with varying skill, essayed his fortune with lance and sword. Some took a liberal proportion of the rings; others merely knocked them over the boundaries, where they were collected by agile little negro boys and handed back to the attendants. A balking horse caused the spectators much amusement and his rider no little chagrin.

The lady who had dropped the handkerchief kept her eye upon the knight who had bound it round his lance. "Who is he, John?" she asked the gentleman beside her.

"That, my dear Rowena, is my good friend and client, George Tryon, of North Carolina. If he had been a stranger, I should have said that he took a liberty; but as things stand, we ought to regard it as a compliment. The incident is quite in accord with the customs of chivalry. If George were but masked and you were veiled, we should have a romantic situation,—you the mysterious damsel in distress, he the unknown champion. The parallel, my dear, might not be so hard to draw, even as things are. But look, it is his turn now; I'll wager that he makes a good run."

"I 'll take you up on that, Mr. Warwick," said Mrs. Newberry from behind, who seemed to have a very keen ear for whatever Warwick said.

Rena's eyes were fastened on her knight, so that she might lose no single one of his movements. As he rode down the lists, more than one woman found him pleasant to look upon. He was a tall, fair young man, with gray eyes, and a frank, open face. He wore a slight mustache, and when he smiled, showed a set of white and even teeth. He was mounted on a very handsome and spirited bay mare, was clad in a picturesque costume, of which velvet knee-breeches and a crimson scarf were the most conspicuous features, and displayed a marked skill in horsemanship. At the blast of the bugle his horse started forward, and, after the first few rods, settled into an even gallop. Tryon's lance, held truly and at the right angle, captured the first ring, then the second and third. His coolness and steadiness seemed not at all disturbed by the applause which followed, and one by one the remaining rings slipped over the point of his lance, until at the end he had taken every one of the twelve. Holding the lance with its booty of captured rings in his left hand, together with the bridle rein, he drew his sabre with the right and rode back over the course. His horse moved like clockwork, his eye was true and his hand steady. Three of the wooden balls fell from the posts, split fairly in the middle, while from the fourth he sliced off a goodly piece and left the remainder standing in its place.

This performance, by far the best up to this point, and barely escaping perfection, elicited a storm of applause. The rider was not so well known to the townspeople as some of the other participants, and his name passed from mouth to mouth in answer to numerous inquiries. The girl whose token he had worn also became an object of renewed interest, because of the result to her in case the knight should prove victor in the contest, of which there could now scarcely be a doubt; for but three riders remained, and it was very improbable that any one of them would excel the last. Wagers for the remainder of the tourney stood anywhere from five, and even from ten to one, in favor of the knight of the crimson sash, and when the last course had been run, his backers were jubilant. No one of those following him had displayed anything like equal skill.

The herald now blew his bugle and declared the tournament closed. The judges put their heads together for a moment. The bugle sounded again, and the herald announced in a loud voice that Sir George Tryon, having taken the greatest number of rings and split the largest number of balls, was proclaimed victor in the tournament and entitled to the flowery chaplet of victory.

Tryon, having bowed repeatedly in response to the liberal applause, advanced to the judges' stand and received the trophy from the hands of the chief judge, who exhorted him to wear the garland worthily, and to yield it only to a better man.

"It will be your privilege, Sir George," announced the judge, "as the chief reward of your valor, to select from the assembled beauty of Clarence the lady whom you wish to honor, to whom we will all do homage as the Queen of Love and Beauty."

Tryon took the wreath and bowed his thanks. Then placing the trophy on the point of his lance, he spoke earnestly for a moment to the herald, and rode past the grand stand, from which there was another outburst of applause. Returning upon his tracks, the knight of the crimson sash paused before the group where Warwick and his sister sat, and lowered the wreath thrice before the lady whose token he had won.

"Oyez! Oyez!" cried the herald; "Sir George Tryon, the victor in the tournament, has chosen Miss Rowena Warwick as the Queen of Love and Beauty, and she will be crowned at the feast to-night and receive the devoirs of all true knights."

The fair-ground was soon covered with scattered groups of the spectators of the tournament. In one group a vanquished knight explained in elaborate detail why it was that he had failed to win the wreath. More than one young woman wondered why some one of the home young men could not have taken the honors, or, if the stranger must win them, why he could not have selected some belle of the town as Queen of Love and Beauty instead of this upstart girl who had blown into the town over night, as one might say.

Warwick and his sister, standing under a spreading elm, held a little court of their own. A dozen gentlemen and several ladies had sought an introduction before Tryon came up.

"I suppose John would have a right to call me out, Miss Warwick," said Tryon, when he had been formally introduced and had shaken hands with Warwick's sister, "for taking liberties with the property and name of a lady to whom I had not had an introduction; but I know John so well that you seemed like an old acquaintance; and when I saw you, and recalled your name, which your brother had mentioned more than once, I felt instinctively that you ought to be the queen. I entered my name only yesterday, merely to swell the number and make the occasion more interesting. These fellows have been practicing for a month, and I had no hope of winning. I should have been satisfied, indeed, if I hadn't made myself ridiculous; but when you dropped your handkerchief, I felt a sudden inspiration; and as soon as I had tied it upon my lance, victory perched upon my saddle-bow, guided my lance and sword, and rings and balls went down before me like chaff before the wind. Oh, it was a great inspiration, Miss Warwick!"

Rena, for it was our Patesville acquaintance fresh from

boarding-school, colored deeply at this frank and fervid flattery, and could only murmur an inarticulate reply. Her year of instruction, while distinctly improving her mind and manners, had scarcely prepared her for so sudden an elevation into a grade of society to which she had hitherto been a stranger. She was not without a certain courage, however, and her brother, who remained at her side, helped her over the most difficult situations.

"We 'll forgive you, George," replied Warwick, "if you'll come home to luncheon with us."

"I'm mighty sorry—awfully sorry," returned Tryon, with evident regret, "but I have another engagement, which I can scarcely break, even by the command of royalty. At what time shall I call for Miss Warwick this evening? I believe that privilege is mine, along with the other honors and rewards of victory,—unless she is bound to some one else."

"She is entirely free," replied Warwick. "Come as early as you like, and I 'll talk to you until she's ready."

Tryon bowed himself away, and after a number of gentlemen and a few ladies had paid their respects to the Queen of Love and Beauty, and received an introduction to her, Warwick signaled to the servant who had his carriage in charge, and was soon driving homeward with his sister. No one of the party noticed a young negro, with a handkerchief bound around his head, who followed them until the carriage turned into the gate and swept up the wide drive that led to Warwick's doorstep.

"Well, Rena," said Warwick, when they found themselves alone, "you have arrived. Your début into society is a little more spectacular than I should have wished, but we must rise to the occasion and make the most of it. You are winning the first fruits of your opportunity. You are the most envied woman in Clarence at this particular moment, and, unless I am mistaken, will be the most admired at the ball to-night."

VI
THE QUEEN OF LOVE AND BEAUTY

SHORTLY after luncheon, Rena had a visitor in the person of Mrs. Newberry, a vivacious young widow of the town, who proffered her services to instruct Rena in the etiquette of the annual ball.

"Now, my dear," said Mrs. Newberry, "the first thing to do is to get your coronation robe ready. It simply means a gown with a long train. You have a lovely white waist. Get right into my buggy, and we'll go down town to get the cloth, take it over to Mrs. Marshall's, and have her run you up a skirt this afternoon."

Rena placed herself unreservedly in the hands of Mrs. Newberry, who introduced her to the best dressmaker of the town, a woman of much experience in such affairs, who improvised during the afternoon a gown suited to the occasion. Mrs. Marshall had made more than a dozen ball dresses during the preceding month; being a wise woman and understanding her business thoroughly, she had made each one of them so that with a few additional touches it might serve for the Queen of Love and Beauty. This was her first direct order for the specific garment.

Tryon escorted Rena to the ball, which was held in the

principal public hall of the town, and attended by all the best people. The champion still wore the costume of the morning, in place of evening dress, save that long stockings and dancing-pumps had taken the place of riding-boots.

Rena went through the ordeal very creditably. Her shyness was palpable, but it was saved from awkwardness by her native grace and good sense. She made up in modesty what she lacked in aplomb. Her months in school had not eradicated a certain self-consciousness born of her secret. The brain-cells never lose the impressions of youth, and Rena's Patesville life was not far enough removed to have lost its distinctness of outline. Of the two, the present was more of a dream, the past was the more vivid reality. At school she had learned something from books and not a little from observation. She had been able to compare herself with other girls, and to see wherein she excelled or fell short of them. With a sincere desire for improvement, and a wish to please her brother and do him credit, she had sought to make the most of her opportunities. Building upon a foundation of innate taste and intelligence, she had acquired much of the self-possession which comes from a knowledge of correct standards of deportment. She had moreover learned without difficulty, for it suited her disposition, to keep silence when she could not speak to advantage. A certain necessary reticence about the past added strength to a natural reserve. Thus equipped, she held her own very well in the somewhat trying ordeal of the ball, at which the fiction of queenship and the attendant ceremonies, which were pretty and graceful, made her the most conspicuous figure. Few of those who watched her move with easy grace through the measures of the dance could have guessed how nearly her heart was in her mouth during much of the time.

"You 're doing splendidly, my dear," said Mrs. Newberry, who had constituted herself Rena's chaperone.

"I trust your Gracious Majesty is pleased with the homage of your devoted subjects," said Tryon, who spent much of his time by her side and kept up the character of knight in his speech and manner.

"Very much," replied the Queen of Love and Beauty, with a somewhat tired smile. It was pleasant, but she would be glad, she thought, when it was all over.

"Keep up your courage," whispered her brother. "You are not only queen, but the belle of the ball. I am proud of you. A dozen women here would give a year off the latter end of life to be in your shoes to-night."

Rena felt immensely relieved when the hour arrived at which she could take her departure, which was to be the signal for the breaking-up of the ball. She was driven home in Tryon's carriage, her brother accompanying them. The night was warm, and the drive homeward under the starlight, in the open carriage, had a soothing effect upon Rena's excited nerves. The calm restfulness of the night, the cool blue depths of the unclouded sky, the solemn croaking of the frogs in a distant swamp, were much more in harmony with her nature than the crowded brilliancy of the ball-room. She closed her eyes, and, leaning back in the carriage, thought of her mother, who she wished might have seen her daughter this night. A momentary pang of homesickness pierced her tender heart, and she furtively wiped away the tears that came into her eyes.

"Good-night, fair Queen!" exclaimed Tryon, breaking into her reverie as the carriage rolled up to the doorstep, "and let your loyal subject kiss your hand in token of his fealty. May your Majesty never abdicate her throne, and may she ever count me her humble servant and devoted knight."

"And now, sister," said Warwick, when Tryon had been driven away, "now that the masquerade is over, let us to sleep, and to-morrow take up the serious business of life. Your day has been a glorious success!"

He put his arm around her and gave her a kiss and a brotherly hug.

"It is a dream," she murmured sleepily, "only a dream. I am Cinderella before the clock has struck. Good-night, dear John."

"Good-night, Rowena."

VII
'MID NEW SURROUNDINGS

WARWICK's residence was situated in the outskirts of the town. It was a fine old plantation house, built in colonial times, with a stately colonnade, wide verandas, and long windows with Venetian blinds. It was painted white, and stood back several rods from the street, in a charming setting of palmettoes, magnolias, and flowering shrubs. Rena had always thought her mother's house large, but now it seemed cramped and narrow, in comparison with this roomy mansion. The furniture was old-fashioned and massive. The great brass andirons on the wide hearth stood like sentinels proclaiming and guarding the dignity of the family. The spreading antlers on the wall testified to a mighty hunter in some past generation. The portraits of Warwick's wife's ancestors—high-featured, proud men and women, dressed in the fashions of a bygone age—looked down from tarnished gilt frames. It was all very novel to her, and very impressive. When she ate off china, with silver knives and forks that had come down as heirlooms, escaping somehow the ravages and exigencies of the war time,—Warwick told her afterwards how he had buried them out of reach of friend or foe,—she thought that her brother must be wealthy, and she felt very proud of him and of her opportunity. The servants, of whom there were several in the house, treated her with a deference to which her eight months in school had only partly accustomed her. At school she had been one of many to be served, and had herself been held to obedience. Here, for the first time in her life, she was mistress, and tasted the sweets of power.

The household consisted of her brother and herself, a cook, a coachman, a nurse, and her brother's little son Albert. The child, with a fine instinct, had put out his puny arms to Rena at first sight, and she had clasped the little man to her bosom with a motherly caress. She had always loved weak creatures. Kittens and puppies had ever found a welcome and a meal at Rena's hands, only to be chased away by Mis' Molly, who had had a wider experience. No shiftless poor white, no half-witted or hungry negro, had ever gone unfed from Mis' Molly's kitchen door if Rena were there to hear his plaint. Little Albert was pale and sickly when she came, but soon bloomed again in the sunshine of her care, and was happy only in her presence. Warwick found pleasure in their growing love for each other, and was glad to perceive that the child formed a living link to connect her with his home.

"Dat chile sutt'nly do lub Miss Rena, an' dat 's a fac', sho 's you bawn," remarked 'Lissa the cook to Mimy the nurse one day. "You'll get yo' nose put out er j'int, ef you don't min'."

"I ain't frettin', honey," laughed the nurse good-naturedly. She was not at all jealous. She had the same wages as before, and her labors were materially lightened by the aunt's attention to the child. This gave Mimy much more time to flirt with Tom the coachman.

It was a source of much gratification to Warwick that his sister seemed to adapt herself so easily to the new conditions. Her graceful movements, the quiet elegance with which she wore even the simplest gown, the easy authoritativeness with which she directed the servants, were to him proofs of superior quality, and he felt correspondingly proud of her. His feeling for her was something more than brotherly love,—he was quite conscious that there were degrees in brotherly love, and that if she had been homely or stupid, he would never have disturbed her in the stagnant life of the house behind the cedars. There had come to him from some source, down the stream of time, a rill of the Greek sense of proportion, of fitness, of beauty, which is indeed but proportion embodied, the perfect adaptation of means to ends. He had perceived, more clearly than she could have appreciated it at that time, the undeveloped elements of discord between Rena and her former life. He had imagined her lending grace and charm to his own household. Still another motive, a purely psychological one, had more or less consciously influenced him. He had no fear that the family secret would ever be discovered,—he had taken his precautions too thoroughly, he thought, for that; and yet he could not but feel, at times, that if perad-venture—it was a conceivable hypothesis—it should be-come known, his fine social position would collapse like a house of cards. Because of this knowledge, which the world around him did not possess, he had felt now and then a certain sense of loneliness; and there was a mea-sure of relief in having about him one who knew his past, and yet whose knowledge, because of their common in-terest, would not interfere with his present or jeopardize his future. For he had always been, in a figurative sense, a naturalized foreigner in the world of wide opportunity, and Rena was one of his old compatriots, whom he was glad to welcome into the populous loneliness of his adopted country.

VIII
THE COURTSHIP

IN a few weeks the echoes of the tournament died away, and Rena's life settled down into a pleasant routine, which she found much more comfortable than her re-cent spectacular prominence. Her queenship, while not entirely forgiven by the ladies of the town, had gained for her a temporary social prominence. Among her own sex, Mrs. Newberry proved a warm and enthusiastic friend. Rumor whispered that the lively young widow would not be unwilling to console Warwick in the loneliness of the old colonial mansion, to which his sister was a most excellent medium of approach. Whether this was true or not it is unnecessary to inquire, for it is no part of this story, except as perhaps indicating why Mrs. Newberry played the part of the female friend, without whom no woman is ever launched successfully in a small and conservative society. Her brother's standing gave her the right of social entry; the tournament opened wide the door, and Mrs. Newberry performed the ceremony of introduction. Rena had many visitors during the month following the tournament, and might have made her choice from among a dozen suitors; but among them all, her knight of the handkerchief found most favor.

George Tryon had come to Clarence a few months before upon business connected with the settlement of his grandfather's estate. A rather complicated litigation had grown up around the affair, various phases of which had kept Tryon almost constantly in the town. He had placed matters in Warwick's hands, and had formed a decided friendship for his attorney, for whom he felt a frank admiration. Tryon was only twenty-three, and his friend's additional five years, supplemented by a certain professional gravity, commanded a great deal of respect from the younger man. When Tryon had known Warwick for a week, he had been ready to swear by him. Indeed, Warwick was a man for whom most people formed a liking at first sight. To this power of attraction he owed most of his success—first with Judge Straight, of Patesville, then with the lawyer whose office he had entered at Clarence, with the woman who became his wife, and with the clients for whom he transacted business. Tryon would have maintained against all comers that Warwick was the finest fellow in the world. When he met Warwick's sister, the foundation for admiration had already been laid. If Rena had proved to be a maiden lady of uncertain age and doubtful personal attractiveness, Tryon would probably have found in her a most excellent lady, worthy of all respect and esteem, and would have treated her with profound deference and sedulous courtesy. When she proved to be a young and handsome woman, of the type that he admired most, he was capable of any degree of infatuation. His mother had for a long time wanted him to marry the orphan daughter of an old friend, a vivacious blonde, who worshiped him. He had felt friendly towards her, but had shrunk from matrimony. He did not want her badly enough to give up his freedom. The war had interfered with his education, and though fairly well instructed, he had never attended college. In his own opinion, he ought to see something of the world, and have his youthful fling. Later on, when he got ready to settle down, if Blanche were still in the humor, they might marry, and sink to the humdrum level of other old married people. The fact that Blanche Leary was visiting his mother during his unexpectedly long absence had not operated at all to hasten his return to North Carolina. He had been having a very good time at Clarence, and, at the distance of several hundred miles, was safe for the time being from any immediate danger of marriage.

With Rena's advent, however, he had seen life through

different glasses. His heart had thrilled at first sight of this tall girl, with the ivory complexion, the rippling brown hair, and the inscrutable eyes. When he became better acquainted with her, he liked to think that her thoughts centred mainly in himself; and in this he was not far wrong. He discovered that she had a short upper lip, and what seemed to him an eminently kissable mouth. After he had dined twice at Warwick's, subsequently to the tournament,—his lucky choice of Rena had put him at once upon a household footing with the family,—his views of marriage changed entirely. It now seemed to him the duty, as well as the high and holy privilege of a young man, to marry and manfully to pay his debt to society. When in Rena's presence, he could not imagine how he had ever contemplated the possibility of marriage with Blanche Leary,—she was utterly, entirely, and hopelessly unsuited to him. For a fair man of vivacious temperament, this stately dark girl was the ideal mate. Even his mother would admit this, if she could only see Rena. To win this beautiful girl for his wife would be a worthy task. He had crowned her Queen of Love and Beauty; since then she had ascended the throne of his heart. He would make her queen of his home and mistress of his life.

To Rena this brief month's courtship came as a new education. Not only had this fair young man crowned her queen, and honored her above all the ladies in town; but since then he had waited assiduously upon her, had spoken softly to her, had looked at her with shining eyes, and had sought to be alone with her. The time soon came when to touch his hand in greeting sent a thrill through her frame,—a time when she listened for his footstep and was happy in his presence. He had been bold enough at the tournament; he had since become somewhat bashful and constrained. He must be in love, she thought, and wondered how soon he would speak. If it were so sweet to walk with him in the garden, or along the shaded streets, to sit with him, to feel the touch of his hand, what happiness would it not be to hear him say that he loved her—to hear his name, to live with him always. To be thus loved and honored by this handsome young man,—she could hardly believe it possible. He would never speak—he would discover her secret and withdraw. She turned pale at the thought,—ah, God! something would happen,—it was too good to be true. The Prince would never try on the glass slipper.

Tryon first told his love for Rena one summer evening on their way home from church. They were walking in the moonlight along the quiet street, which, but for their presence, seemed quite deserted.

"Miss Warwick—Rowena," he said, clasping with his right hand the hand that rested on his left arm, "I love you! Do you—love me?"

To Rena this simple avowal came with much greater force than a more formal declaration could have had. It appealed to her own simple nature. Indeed, few women at such a moment criticise the form in which the most fateful words of life—but one—are spoken. Words, while pleasant, are really superfluous. Her whispered "Yes" spoke volumes.

They walked on past the house, along the country road into which the street soon merged. When they returned, an hour later, they found Warwick seated on the piazza, in a rocking-chair, smoking a fragrant cigar.

"Well, children," he observed with mock severity, "you are late in getting home from church. The sermon must have been extremely long."

"We have been attending an after-meeting," replied Tryon joyfully, "and have been discussing an old text, 'Little children, love one another,' and its corollary, 'It is not good for man to live alone.' John, I am the happiest man alive. Your sister has promised to marry me. I should like to shake my brother's hand."

Never does one feel so strongly the universal brotherhood of man as when one loves some other fellow's sister. Warwick sprang from his chair and clasped Tryon's extended hand with real emotion. He knew of no man whom he would have preferred to Tryon as a husband for his sister.

"My dear George—my dear sister," he exclaimed, "I am very, very glad. I wish you every happiness. My sister is the most fortunate of women."

"And I am the luckiest of men," cried Tryon.

"I wish you every happiness," repeated Warwick; adding, with a touch of solemnity, as a certain thought, never far distant, occurred to him, "I hope that neither of you may ever regret your choice."

Thus placed upon the footing of an accepted lover, Tryon's visits to the house became more frequent. He wished to fix a time for the marriage, but at this point Rena developed a strange reluctance.

"Can we not love each other for a while?" she asked. "To be engaged is a pleasure that comes but once; it would be a pity to cut it too short."

"It is a pleasure that I would cheerfully dispense with," he replied, "for the certainty of possession. I want you all to myself, and all the time. Things might happen. If I should die, for instance, before I married you"—

"Oh, don't suppose such awful things," she cried, putting her hand over his mouth.

He held it there and kissed it until she pulled it away.

"I should consider," he resumed, completing the sentence, "that my life had been a failure."

"If I should die," she murmured, "I should die happy in the knowledge that you had loved me."

"In three weeks," he went on, "I shall have finished my business in Clarence, and there will be but one thing to keep me here. When shall it be? I must take you home with me."

"I will let you know," she replied, with a troubled sigh, "in a week from to-day."

"I'll call your attention to the subject every day in the mean time," he asserted. "I should n't like you to forget it."

Rena's shrinking from the irrevocable step of marriage was due to a simple and yet complex cause. Stated baldly, it was the consciousness of her secret; the complexity arose out of the various ways in which it seemed to bear upon her future. Our lives are so bound up with those of our fellow men that the slightest departure from the beaten path involves a multiplicity of small adjustments. It had not been difficult for Rena to conform her speech, her manners, and in a measure her modes of thought, to those of the people around her; but when this readjustment went beyond mere externals and concerned the vital issues of life, the secret that oppressed her took on a more serious aspect, with tragic possibilities. A discursive imagination was not one of her characteristics, or the danger of a marriage of which perfect frankness was not a condition might well have presented itself before her heart had become involved. Under the influence of doubt and fear acting upon love, the invisible bar to happiness glowed with a lambent flame that threatened dire disaster.

"Would he have loved me at all," she asked herself, "if he had known the story of my past? Or, having loved me, could he blame me now for what I cannot help?"

There were two shoals in the channel of her life, upon either of which her happiness might go to shipwreck. Since leaving the house behind the cedars, where she had been brought into the world without her own knowledge or consent, and had first drawn the breath of life by the involuntary contraction of certain muscles, Rena had learned, in a short time, many things; but she was yet to learn that the innocent suffer with the guilty, and feel the punishment the more keenly because unmerited. She had yet to learn that the old Mosaic formula, "The sins of the fathers shall be visited upon the children," was graven more indelibly upon the heart of the race than upon the tables of Sinai.

But would her lover still love her, if he knew all? She had read some of the novels in the bookcase in her mother's hall, and others at boarding-school. She had read that love was a conqueror, that neither life nor death, nor creed nor caste, could stay his triumphant course. Her secret was no legal bar to their union. If Rena could forget the secret, and Tryon should never know it, it would be no obstacle to their happiness. But Rena felt, with a sinking of the heart, that happiness was not a matter of law or of fact, but lay entirely within the domain of sentiment. We are happy when we think ourselves happy, and with a strange perversity we often differ from others with regard to what should constitute our happiness. Rena's secret was the worm in the bud, the skeleton in the closet.

"He says that he loves me. He *does* love me. Would he love me, if he knew?" She stood before an oval mirror brought from France by one of Warwick's wife's ancestors, and regarded her image with a coldly critical eye. She was as little vain as any of her sex who are endowed with beauty. She tried to place herself, in thus passing upon her own claims to consideration, in the hostile attitude of society toward her hidden disability. There was no mark upon her brow to brand her as less pure, less innocent, less desirable, less worthy to be loved, than these proud women of the past who had admired themselves in this old mirror.

"I think a man might love me for myself," she murmured pathetically, "and if he loved me truly, that he would marry me. If he would not marry me, then it would be because he did n't love me. I'll tell George my secret. If he leaves me, then he does not love me."

But this resolution vanished into thin air before it was fully formulated. The secret was not hers alone; it involved her brother's position, to whom she owed everything, and in less degree the future of her little nephew, whom she had learned to love so well. She had the choice of but two courses of action, to marry Tryon or to dismiss him. The thought that she might lose him made him seem only more dear; to think that he might leave her made her sick at heart. In one week she was bound to give him an answer; he was more likely to ask for it at their next meeting.

IX
DOUBTS AND FEARS

RENA's heart was too heavy with these misgivings for her to keep them to herself. On the morning after the conversation with Tryon in which she had promised him an answer within a week, she went into her brother's study, where he usually spent an hour after breakfast before going to his office. He looked up amiably from the book before him and read trouble in her face.

"Well, Rena, dear," he asked with a smile, "what's the matter? Is there anything you want—money, or what? I should like to have Aladdin's lamp—though I'd hardly need it—that you might have no wish unsatisfied."

He had found her very backward in asking for things that she needed. Generous with his means, he thought nothing too good for her. Her success had gratified his pride, and justified his course in taking her under his protection.

"Thank you, John. You give me already more than I need. It is something else, John. George wants me to say when I will marry him. I am afraid to marry him, without telling him. If he should find out afterwards, he might cast me off, or cease to love me. If he did not know it, I should be forever thinking of what he would do if he *should* find it out; or, if I should die without his having learned it, I should not rest easy in my grave for thinking of what he would have done if he *had* found it out."

Warwick's smile gave place to a grave expression at this somewhat comprehensive statement. He rose and closed the door carefully, lest some one of the servants might overhear the conversation. More liberally endowed than

Rena with imagination, and not without a vein of sentiment, he had nevertheless a practical side that out-
weighed them both. With him, the problem that oppressed his sister had been in the main a matter of argument, of self-conviction. Once persuaded that he had
certain rights, or ought to have them, by virtue of the
laws of nature, in defiance of the customs of mankind,
he had promptly sought to enjoy them. This he had been
able to do by simply concealing his antecedents and making the most of his opportunities, with no troublesome
qualms of conscience whatever. But he had already perceived, in their brief intercourse, that Rena's emotions,
while less easily stirred, touched a deeper note than his,
and dwelt upon it with greater intensity than if they had
been spread over the larger field to which a more ready
sympathy would have supplied so many points of ac-
cess;—hers was a deep and silent current flowing between the narrow walls of a self-contained life, his the
spreading river that ran through a pleasant landscape.
Warwick's imagination, however, enabled him to put himself in touch with her mood and recognize its bearings
upon her conduct. He would have preferred her taking
the practical point of view, to bring her round to which
he perceived would be a matter of diplomacy.

"How long have these weighty thoughts been trou-
bling your small head?" he asked with assumed lightness.

"Since he asked me last night to name our wedding
day."

"My dear child," continued Warwick, "you take too
tragic a view of life. Marriage is a reciprocal arrangement,
by which the contracting parties give love for love, care
for keeping, faith for faith. It is a matter of the future,

not of the past. What a poor soul it is that has not some secret chamber, sacred to itself; where one can file away the things others have no right to know, as well as things that one himself would fain forget! We are under no moral obligation to inflict upon others the history of our past mistakes, our wayward thoughts, our secret sins, our desperate hopes, or our heartbreaking disappointments. Still less are we bound to bring out from this secret chamber the dusty record of our ancestry.

'Let the dead past bury its dead.'

George Tryon loves you for yourself alone; it is not your ancestors that he seeks to marry."

"But would be marry me if he knew?" she persisted.

Warwick paused for reflection. He would have preferred to argue the question in a general way, but felt the necessity of satisfying her scruples, as far as might be. He had liked Tryon from the very beginning of their acquaintance. In all their intercourse, which had been very close for several months, he had been impressed by the young man's sunny temper, his straightforwardness, his intellectual honesty. Tryon's deference to Warwick as the elder man had very naturally proved an attraction. Whether this friendship would have stood the test of utter frankness about his own past was a merely academic speculation with which Warwick did not trouble himself. With his sister the question had evidently become a matter of conscience,—a difficult subject with which to deal in a person of Rena's temperament.

"My dear sister," he replied, "why should he know? We have n't asked him for his pedigree; we don't care to know it. If he cares for ours, he should ask for it, and it would then be time enough to raise the question. You love him, I imagine, and wish to make him happy?"

It is the highest wish of the woman who loves. The enamored man seeks his own happiness; the loving woman finds no sacrifice too great for the loved one. The fiction of chivalry made man serve woman; the fact of human nature makes woman happiest when serving where she loves.

"Yes, oh, yes," Rena exclaimed with fervor, clasping her hands unconsciously. "I'm afraid he 'd be unhappy if he knew, and it would make me miserable to think him unhappy."

"Well, then," said Warwick, "suppose we should tell him our secret and put ourselves in his power, and that he should then conclude that he could n't marry you? Do you imagine he would be any happier than he is now, or than if he should never know?"

Ah, no! she could not think so. One could not tear love out of one's heart without pain and suffering.

There was a knock at the door. Warwick opened it to the nurse, who stood with little Albert in her arms.

"Please, suh," said the girl, with a curtsy, "de baby's be'n cryin' an' frettin' fer Miss Rena, an' I 'lowed she mought want me ter fetch 'im, ef it would n't 'sturb, her."

"Give me the darling," exclaimed Rena, coming forward and taking the child from the nurse. "It wants its auntie. Come to its auntie, bless its little heart!"

Little Albert crowed with pleasure and put up his pretty mouth for a kiss. Warwick found the sight a pleasant one. If he could but quiet his sister's troublesome scruples, he might erelong see her fondling beautiful children of her own. Even if Rena were willing to risk her happiness, and he to endanger his position, by a quixotic frankness, the future of his child must not be compromised.

"You would n't want to make George unhappy," Warwick resumed when the nurse retired. "Very well; would you not be willing, for his sake, to keep a secret— your secret and mine, and that of the innocent child in your arms? Would you involve all of us in difficulties merely to secure your own peace of mind? Does n't such a course seem just the least bit selfish? Think the matter over from that point of view, and we'll speak of it later in the day. I shall be with George all the morning, and I may be able, by a little management, to find out his views on the subject of birth and family, and all that. Some men are very liberal, and love is a great leveler. I'll sound him, at any rate."

He kissed the baby and left Rena to her own reflections, to which his presentation of the case had given a new turn. It had never before occurred to her to regard silence in the light of self-sacrifice. It had seemed a sort of sin; her brother's argument made of it a virtue. It was not the first time, nor the last, that right and wrong had been a matter of view-point.

Tryon himself furnished the opening for Warwick's proposed examination. The younger man could not long remain silent upon the subject uppermost in his mind. "I am anxious, John," he said, "to have Rowena name the happiest day of my life—our wedding day. When the trial in Edgecombe County is finished, I shall have no further business here, and shall be ready to leave for home. I should like to take my bride with me, and surprise my mother."

Mothers, thought Warwick, are likely to prove inquisitive about their sons' wives, especially when taken unawares in matters of such importance. This seemed a good time to test the liberality of Tryon's views, and to put forward a shield for his sister's protection.

"Are you sure, George, that your mother will find the surprise agreeable when you bring home a bride of whom you know so little and your mother nothing at all?"

Tryon had felt that it would be best to surprise his mother. She would need only to see Rena to approve of her, but she was so far prejudiced in favor of Blanche Leary that it would be wisest to present the argument after having announced the irrevocable conclusion. Rena herself would be a complete justification for the accomplished deed.

"I think you ought to know, George," continued Warwick, without waiting for a reply to his question, "that my sister and I are not of an old family, or a rich family, or a distinguished family; that she can bring you nothing but herself; that we have no connections of which you could boast, and no relatives to whom we should be glad to introduce you. You must take us for ourselves alone—we are new people."

"My dear John," replied the young man warmly, "there is a great deal of nonsense about families. If a man is noble and brave and strong, if a woman is beautiful and good and true, what matters it about his or her ancestry? If an old family can give them these things, then it is valuable; if they possess them without it, then of what use is it, except as a source of empty pride, which they would be better without? If all new families were like yours, there would be no advantage in belonging to an old one. All I care to know of Rowena's family is that she is your sister; and you'll pardon me, old fellow, if I add that she hardly needs even you,—she carries the stamp of her descent upon her face and in her heart."

"It makes me glad to hear you speak in that way," returned Warwick, delighted by the young man's breadth and earnestness.

"Oh, I mean every word of it," replied Tryon. "Ancestors, indeed, for Rowena! I will tell you a family secret, John, to prove how little I am for ancestors. My maternal great-great-grandfather, a hundred and fifty years ago, was hanged, drawn, and quartered for stealing cattle across the Scottish border. How is that for a pedigree? Behold in me the lineal descendant of a felon!"

Warwick felt much relieved at this avowal. His own statement had not touched the vital point involved; it had been at the best but a half-truth; but Tryon's magnanimity would doubtless protect Rena from any close inquiry concerning her past. It even occurred to Warwick for a moment that he might safely disclose the secret to Tryon; but an appreciation of certain facts of history and certain traits of human nature constrained him to put the momentary thought aside. It was a great relief, however, to imagine that Tryon might think lightly of this thing that he need never know.

"Well, Rena," he said to his sister when he went home at noon: "I've sounded George."

"What did he say?" she asked eagerly.

"I told him we were people of no family, and that we had no relatives that we were proud of. He said he loved you for yourself, and would never ask you about your ancestry."

"Oh, I am so glad!" exclaimed Rena joyfully. This report left her very happy for about three hours, or until she began to analyze carefully her brother's account of what had been said. Warwick's statement had not been specific,—he had not told Tryon *the* thing. George's reply, in turn, had been a mere generality. The concrete fact that oppressed her remained unrevealed, and her doubt was still unsatisfied.

Rena was occupied with this thought when her lover next came to see her. Tryon came up the sanded walk from the gate and spoke pleasantly to the nurse, a good-looking yellow girl who was seated on the front steps, playing with little Albert, He took the boy from her arms, and she went to call Miss Warwick.

Rena came out, followed by the nurse, who offered to take the child.

"Never mind, Mimy, leave him with me," said Tryon.

The nurse walked discreetly over into the garden, remaining within call, but beyond the hearing of conversation in an ordinary tone.

"Rena, darling," said her lover, "when shall it be? Surely you won't ask me to wait a week. Why, that's a lifetime!"

Rena was struck by a brilliant idea. She would test her lover. Love was a very powerful force; she had found it the greatest, grandest, sweetest thing in the world. Tryon had said that he loved her; he had said scarcely anything else for several weeks, surely nothing else worth remembering. She would test his love by a hypothetical question.

"You say you love me," she said, glancing at him with a sad thoughtfulness in her large dark eyes. "How much do you love me?"

"I love you all one can love. True love has no degrees; it is all or nothing!"

"Would you love me," she asked, with an air of coquetry that masked her concern, pointing toward the girl in the shrubbery, "if I were Albert's nurse yonder?"

"If you were Albert's nurse," he replied, with a joyous laugh, "he would have to find another within a week, for within a week we should be married."

The answer seemed to fit the question, but in fact, Tryon's mind and Rena's did not meet. That two intelligent persons should each attach a different meaning to so simple a form of words as Rena's question was the best ground for her misgiving with regard to the marriage. But love blinded her. She was anxious to be convinced. She interpreted the meaning of his speech by her own thought and by the ardor of his glance, and was satisfied with the answer.

"And now, darling," pleaded Tryon, "will you not fix the day that shall make me happy? I shall be ready to go away in three weeks. Will you go with me?"

"Yes," she answered, in a tumult of joy. She would never need to tell him her secret now. It would make no difference with him, so far as she was concerned; and she had no right to reveal her brother's secret. She was willing to bury the past in forgetfulness, now that she knew it would have no interest for her lover.

X
THE DREAM

THE marriage was fixed for the thirtieth of the month, immediately after which Tryon and his bride were to set out for North Carolina. Warwick would have liked it much if Tryon had lived in South Carolina; but the location of his North Carolina home was at some distance from Patesville, with which it had no connection by steam or rail, and indeed lay altogether out of the line of travel to Patesville. Rena had no acquaintance with people of social standing in North Carolina; and with the added maturity and charm due to her improved opportunities, it was unlikely that any former resident of Patesville who might casually meet her would see in the elegant young matron from South Carolina more than a passing resemblance to a poor girl who had once lived in an obscure part of the old town. It would of course be necessary for Rena to keep away from Patesville; save for her mother's sake, she would hardly be tempted to go back.

On the twentieth of the month, Warwick set out with Tryon for the county seat of the adjoining county, to try one of the lawsuits which had required Tryon's presence in South Carolina for so long a time. Their destination was a day's drive from Clarence, behind a good horse, and the trial was expected to last a week.

"This week will seem like a year," said Tryon ruefully, the evening before their departure, "but I'll write every day, and shall expect a letter as often."

"The mail goes only twice a week, George," replied Rena.

"Then I shall have three letters in each mail."

Warwick and Tryon were to set out in the cool of the morning, after an early breakfast. Rena was up at daybreak that she might preside at the breakfast-table and bid the travelers good-by.

"John," said Rena to her brother in the morning, "I dreamed last night that mother was ill."

"Dreams, you know, Rena," answered Warwick lightly, "go by contraries. Yours undoubtedly signifies that our mother, God bless her simple soul! is at the present moment enjoying her usual perfect health. She was never sick in her life."

For a few months after leaving Patesville with her brother, Rena had suffered tortures of home-sickness; those who have felt it know the pang. The severance of old ties had been abrupt and complete. At the school where her brother had taken her, there had been nothing to relieve the strangeness of her surroundings—no schoolmate from her own town, no relative or friend of the family near by. Even the compensation of human sympathy was in a measure denied her, for Rena was too fresh from her prison-house to doubt that sympathy would fail before the revelation of the secret the consciousness of which oppressed her at that time like a nightmare. It was not strange that Rena, thus isolated, should have been prostrated by homesickness for several weeks after leaving Patesville. When the paroxysm had passed, there followed a dull pain, which gradually subsided into a resignation as profound, in its way, as had been her longing for home. She loved, she suffered, with a quiet intensity of which her outward demeanor gave no adequate expression. From some ancestral source she had derived a strain of the passive fatalism by which alone one can submit uncomplainingly to the inevitable. By the same token, when once a thing had been decided, it became with her a finality, which only some extraordinary stress of emotion could disturb. She had acquiesced in her brother's plan; for her there was no withdrawing; her homesickness was an incidental thing which must be endured, as patiently as might be, until time should have brought a measure of relief.

Warwick had made provision for an occasional letter from Patesville, by leaving with his mother a number of envelopes directed to his address. She could have her letters written, inclose them in these envelopes, and deposit them in the post-office with her own hand. Thus the place of Warwick's residence would remain within her own knowledge, and his secret would not be placed at the mercy of any wandering Patesvillian who might perchance go to that part of South Carolina. By this simple means Rena had kept as closely in touch with her mother as Warwick had considered prudent; any closer intercourse was not consistent with their present station in life.

The night after Warwick and Tryon had ridden away, Rena dreamed again that her mother was ill. Better taught people than she, in regions more enlightened than the South Carolina of that epoch, are disturbed at times by dreams. Mis' Molly had a profound faith in them. If God, in ancient times, had spoken to men in visions of the night, what easier way could there be for Him to convey his meaning to people of all ages? Science, which has shattered many an idol and destroyed many a delusion, has made but slight inroads upon the shadowy realm of dreams. For Mis' Molly, to whom science would have meant nothing and psychology would have been a meaningless term, the land of dreams was carefully mapped and bounded. Each dream had some special significance, or was at least susceptible of classification under some significant head. Dreams, as a general rule, went by contraries; but a dream three times repeated was a certain portent of the thing defined. Rena's few years of schooling at Patesville and her months at Charleston had scarcely disturbed these hoary superstitions which lurk in the dim corners of the brain. No lady in Clarence, perhaps, would have remained undisturbed by a vivid dream, three times repeated, of some event bearing materially upon her own life.

The first repetition of a dream was decisive of nothing, for two dreams meant no more than one. The power of the second lay in the suspense, the uncertainty, to which it gave rise. Two doubled the chance of a third. The day following this second dream was an anxious one for Rena. She could not for an instant dismiss her mother from her thoughts, which were filled too with a certain self-reproach. She had left her mother alone; if her mother were really ill, there was no one at home to tend her with loving care. This feeling grew in force, until by nightfall Rena had become very unhappy, and went to bed with the most dismal forebodings. In this state of mind, it is not surprising that she now dreamed that her mother was lying at the point of death, and that she cried out with heart-rending pathos:—

"Rena, my darlin', why did you forsake yo'r pore old mother? Come back to me, honey; I'll die ef I don't see you soon."

The stress of subconscious emotion engendered by the dream was powerful enough to wake Rena, and her mother's utterance seemed to come to her with the force of a fateful warning and a great reproach. Her mother was sick and needed her, and would die if she did not come. She felt that she must see her mother,—it would be almost like murder to remain away from her under such circumstances.

After breakfast she went into the business part of the town and inquired at what time a train would leave that would take her toward Patesville. Since she had come away from the town, a railroad had been opened by which the long river voyage might be avoided, and, making allowance for slow trains and irregular connections, the town of Patesville could be reached by an all-rail route in about twelve hours. Calling at the post-office for the family mail, she found there a letter from her mother, which she tore open in great excitement. It was written in an unpracticed hand and badly spelled, and was in effect as follows:—

My dear Daughter,—I take my pen in hand to let you know that I am not very well. I have had a kind of misery in my side for two weeks, with palpitations of the heart, and I have been in bed for three days. I 'm feeling mighty poorly, but Dr. Green says that I 'll get over it in a few days. Old Aunt Zilphy is staying with me, and looking after things tolerably well. I hope this will find you and John enjoying good health. Give my love to John, and I hope the Lord will bless him and you too. Cousin Billy Oxendine has had a rising on his neck, and has had to have it lanced. Mary B. has another young one, a boy this time. Old man Tom Johnson was killed last week while trying to whip black Jim Brown, who lived down on the Wilmington Road. Jim has run away. There has been a big freshet in the river, and it looked at one time as if the new bridge would be washed away.

Frank comes over every day or two and asks about you. He says to tell you that he don't believe you are coming back any more, but you are to remember him, and that foolishness he said about bringing you back from the end of the world with his mule and cart. He 's very good to me, and brings over shavings and kindling-wood, and made me a new well-bucket for nothing. It's a comfort to talk to him about you, though I have n't told him where you are living.

I hope this will find you and John both well, and doing well. I should like to see you, but if it's the Lord's will that I should n't, I shall be thankful anyway that you have done what was the best for yourselves and your children, and that I have given you up for your own good.

Your affectionate mother,
MARY WALDEN.

Rena shed tears over this simple letter, which, to her excited imagination, merely confirmed the warning of her dream. At the date of its writing her mother had been sick in bed, with the symptoms of a serious illness. She had no nurse but a purblind old woman. Three days of progressive illness had evidently been quite sufficient to reduce her parent to the condition indicated by the third dream. The thought that her mother might die without the presence of any one who loved her pierced Rena's heart like a knife and lent wings to her feet. She wished for the enchanted horse of which her brother had read to her so many years before on the front piazza of the house behind the cedars, that she might fly through the air to her dying mother's side. She determined to go at once to Patesville.

Returning home, she wrote a letter to Warwick inclosing their mother's letter, and stating that she had dreamed an alarming dream for three nights in succession; that she had left the house in charge of the servants and gone to Patesville; and that she would return as soon as her mother was out of danger.

To her lover she wrote that she had been called away to visit a sick-bed, and would return very soon, perhaps by the time he got back to Clarence. These letters Rena posted on her way to the train, which she took at five o'clock in the afternoon. This would bring her to Patesville early in the morning of the following day.

XI
A LETTER AND A JOURNEY

WAR has been called the court of last resort. A lawsuit may with equal aptness be compared to a battle—the parallel might be drawn very closely all along the line. First we have the *casus belli*, the cause of action; then the various protocols and proclamations and general orders, by way of pleas, demurrers, and motions; then the preliminary skirmishes at the trial table; and then the final struggle, in which might is quite as likely to prevail

as right, victory most often resting with the strongest bat-
talions, and truth and justice not seldom overborne by
the weight of odds upon the other side.

The lawsuit which Warwick and Tryon had gone to try
did not, however, reach this ultimate stage, but, after a
three days' engagement, resulted in a treaty of peace.
The case was compromised and settled, and Tryon and
Warwick set out on their homeward drive. They stopped
at a farmhouse at noon, and while at table saw the stage-
coach from the town they had just left, bound for their
own destination. In the mail-bag under the driver's seat
were Rena's two letters; they had been delivered at the
town in the morning, and immediately remailed to
Clarence, in accordance with orders left at the post-office the evening before. Tryon and Warwick drove leisurely homeward through the pines, all unconscious of
the fateful squares of white paper moving along the road
a few miles before them, which a mother's yearning and
a daughter's love had thrown, like the apple of discord,
into the narrow circle of their happiness.

They reached Clarence at four o'clock. Warwick got
down from the buggy at his office. Tryon drove on to his
hotel, to make a hasty toilet before visiting his sweetheart.

Warwick glanced at his mail, tore open the envelope
addressed in his sister's handwriting, and read the contents with something like dismay. She had gone away on
the eve of her wedding, her lover knew not where, to be
gone no one knew how long, on a mission which could
not be frankly disclosed. A dim foreboding of disaster
flashed across his mind. He thrust the letter into his
pocket, with others yet unopened, and started toward his
home. Reaching the gate, he paused a moment and then

walked on past the house. Tryon would probably be there in a few minutes, and he did not care to meet him without first having had the opportunity for some moments of reflection. He must fix upon some line of action in this emergency.

Meanwhile Tryon had reached his hotel and opened his mail. The letter from Rena was read first, with profound disappointment. He had really made concessions in the settlement of that lawsuit—had yielded several hundred dollars of his just dues, in order that he might get back to Rena three days earlier. Now he must cool his heels in idleness for at least three days before she would return. It was annoying, to say the least. He wished to know where she had gone, that he might follow her and stay near her until she should be ready to come back. He might ask Warwick—no, she might have had some good reason for not having mentioned her destination. She had probably gone to visit some of the poor relations of whom her brother had spoken so frankly, and she would doubtless prefer that he should not see her amid any surroundings but the best. Indeed, he did not know that he would himself care to endanger, by suggestive comparisons, the fine aureole of superiority that surrounded her. She represented in her adorable person and her pure heart the finest flower of the finest race that God had ever made—the supreme effort of creative power, than which there could be no finer. The flower would soon be his; why should he care to dig up the soil in which it grew?

Tryon went on opening his letters. There were several bills and circulars, and then a letter from his mother, of which he broke the seal:—

My dearest George,—This leaves us well. Blanche is still with me, and we are impatiently awaiting your return. In your absence she seems almost like a daughter to me. She joins me in the hope that your lawsuits are progressing favorably, and that you will be with us soon. . . .

On your way home, if it does not keep you away from us too long, would it not be well for you to come by way of Patesville, and find out whether there is any prospect of our being able to collect our claim against old Mr. Duncan McSwayne's estate? You must have taken the papers with you, along with the rest, for I do not find them here. Things ought to be settled enough now for people to realize on some of their securities. Your grandfather always believed the note was good, and meant to try to collect it, but the war interfered. He said to me, before he died, that if the note was ever collected, he would use the money to buy a wedding present for your wife. Poor father! he is dead and gone to heaven; but I am sure that even there he would be happier if he knew the note was paid and the money used as he intended.

If you go to Patesville, call on my cousin, Dr. Ed. Green, and tell him who you are. Give him my love. I have n't seen him for twenty years. He used to be very fond of the ladies, a very gallant man. He can direct you to a good lawyer, no doubt. Hoping to see you soon,

Your loving mother,
Elizabeth Tryon.

P. S. Blanche joins me in love to you.

This affectionate and motherly letter did not give Tryon unalloyed satisfaction. He was glad to hear that his mother was well, but he had hoped that Blanche Leary might have finished her visit by this time. The reasonable inference from the letter was that Blanche meant to await his return. Her presence would spoil the fine romantic flavor of the surprise he had planned for his mother; it would never do to expose his bride to an unannounced meeting with the woman whom he had tacitly rejected. There would be one advantage in such a meeting: the comparison of the two women would be so much in Rena's favor that his mother could not hesitate for a moment between them. The situation, however, would have elements of constraint, and he did not care to expose either Rena or Blanche to any disagreeable contingency. It would be better to take his wife on a wedding trip, and notify his mother, before he returned home, of his marriage. In the extremely improbable case that she should disapprove his choice after having seen his wife, the ice would at least have been broken before his arrival at home.

"By Jove!" he exclaimed suddenly, striking his knee with his hand, "why should n't I run up to Patesville while Rena's gone? I can leave here at five o'clock, and get there some time to-morrow morning. I can transact my business during the day, and get back the day after to-morrow; for Rena might return ahead of time, just as we did, and I shall want to be here when she comes; I'd rather wait a year for a legal opinion on a doubtful old note than to lose one day with my love. The train goes in twenty minutes. My bag is already packed. I'll just drop a line to George and tell him where I've gone."

He put Rena's letter into his breast pocket, and turning to his trunk, took from it a handful of papers relating to the claim in reference to which he was going to Patesville. These he thrust into the same pocket with Rena's letter; he wished to read both letter and papers while on the train. It would be a pleasure merely to hold the letter before his eyes and look at the lines traced by her hand. The papers he wished to study, for the more practical purpose of examining into the merits of his claim against the estate of Duncan McSwayne.

When Warwick reached home, he inquired if Mr. Tryon had called.

"No, suh," answered the nurse, to whom he had put the question; "he ain't be'n here yet, suh."

Warwick was surprised and much disturbed.

"De baby's be'n cryin' for Miss Rena," suggested the nurse, "an' I s'pec' he'd like to see you, suh. Shall I fetch 'im?"

"Yes, bring him to me."

He took the child in his arms and went out upon the piazza. Several porch pillows lay invitingly near. He pushed them toward the steps with his foot, sat down upon one, and placed little Albert upon another. He was scarcely seated when a messenger from the hotel came up the walk from the gate and handed him a note. At the same moment he heard the long shriek of the afternoon train leaving the station on the opposite side of the town.

He tore the envelope open anxiously, read the note, smiled a sickly smile, and clenched the paper in his hand unconsciously. There was nothing he could do. The train had gone; there was no telegraph to Patesville, and no letter could leave Clarence for twenty-four hours. The best laid schemes go wrong at times—the stanchest ships are sometimes wrecked, or skirt the breakers perilously. Life is a sea, full of strange currents and uncharted reefs—whoever leaves the traveled path must run the danger of destruction. Warwick was a lawyer, however, and accustomed to balance probabilities.

"He may easily be in Patesville a day or two without meeting her. She will spend most of her time at mother's bedside, and he will be occupied with his own affairs."

If Tryon should meet her—well, he was very much in love, and he had spoken very nobly of birth and blood. Warwick would have preferred, nevertheless, that Tryon's theories should not be put to this particular test. Rena's scruples had so far been successfully combated; the question would be opened again, and the situation unnecessarily complicated, if Tryon should meet Rena in Patesville.

"Will he or will he not?" he asked himself. He took a coin from his pocket and spun it upon the floor. "Heads, he sees her; tails, he does not."

The coin spun swiftly and steadily, leaving upon the eye the impression of a revolving sphere. Little Albert, left for a moment to his own devices, had crept behind his father and was watching the whirling disk with great pleasure. He felt that he would like to possess this interesting object. The coin began to move more slowly, and was wabbling to its fall, when the child stretched forth his chubby fist and caught it ere it touched the floor.

XII
TRYON GOES TO PATESVILLE

Tryon arrived in the early morning and put up at the Patesville Hotel, a very comfortable inn. After a bath, breakfast, and a visit to the barbershop, he inquired of the hotel clerk the way to the office of Dr. Green, his mother's cousin.

"On the corner, sir," answered the clerk, "by the market-house, just over the drugstore. The doctor drove past here only half an hour ago. You 'll probably catch him in his office."

Tryon found the office without difficulty. He climbed the stair, but found no one in except a young colored man seated in the outer office, who rose promptly as Tryon entered.

"No, suh," replied the man to Tryon's question, "he ain't hyuh now. He 's gone out to see a patient, suh, but he'll be back soon. Won't you set down in de private office an' wait fer 'im, suh?"

Tryon had not slept well during his journey, and felt somewhat fatigued. Through the open door of the next room he saw an inviting armchair, with a window at one side, and upon the other a table strewn with papers and magazines.

"Yes," he answered, "I 'll wait."

He entered the private office, sank into the arm-chair, and looked out of the window upon the square below. The view was mildly interesting. The old brick market-house with the tower was quite picturesque. On a wagon-scale at one end the public weighmaster was weighing a load of hay. In the booths under the wide arches several old negro women were frying fish on little charcoal stoves—the odor would have been appetizing to one who had not breakfasted. On the shady side stood half a dozen two-wheeled carts, loaded with lightwood and drawn by diminutive steers, or superannuated army mules branded on the flank with the cabalistic letters "C.S.A.," which represented a vanished dream, or "U. S. A.," which, as any negro about the market-house would have borne witness, signified a very concrete fact. Now and then a lady or gentleman passed with leisurely step—no one ever hurried in Patesville—or some poor white sandhiller slouched listlessly along toward store or bar-room.

Tryon mechanically counted the slabs of ginger-bread on the nearest market-stall, and calculated the cubical contents of several of the meagre loads of wood. Having exhausted the view, he turned to the table at his elbow and picked up a medical journal, in which he read first an account of a marvelous surgical operation. Turning the leaves idly, he came upon an article by a Southern writer, upon the perennial race problem that has vexed the country for a century. The writer maintained that owing to a special tendency of the negro blood, however diluted, to revert to the African type, any future amalgamation of the white and black races, which foolish and wicked Northern negrophiles predicted as the ultimate result of the new conditions confronting the South, would therefore be an ethnological impossibility; for the smallest trace of negro blood would inevitably drag down the superior race to the level of the inferior, and reduce the fair Southland, already devastated by the hand of the invader, to the frightful level of Hayti, the awful example of negro incapacity. To forefend their beloved land, now doubly sanctified by the blood of her devoted sons who had fallen in the struggle to maintain her liberties and preserve her property, it behooved every true Southron to stand firm against the abhorrent tide of radicalism, to maintain the supremacy and purity of his all-pervading, all-conquering race, and to resist by every available means the threatened domination of an inferior and degraded people, who were set to rule hereditary freemen ere they had themselves scarce ceased to be slaves.

When Tryon had finished the article, which seemed to him a well-considered argument, albeit a trifle bombastic, he threw the book upon the table. Finding the armchair wonderfully comfortable, and feeling the fatigue of his journey, he yielded to a drowsy impulse, leaned his head on the cushioned back of the chair, and fell asleep. According to the habit of youth, he dreamed, and pursuant to his own individual habit, he dreamed of Rena. They were walking in the moonlight, along the quiet road in front of her brother's house. The air was redolent with the perfume of flowers. His arm was around her waist. He had asked her if she loved him, and was awaiting her answer in tremulous but confident expectation. She opened her lips to speak. The sound that came from them seemed to be:—

"Is Dr. Green in? No? Ask him, when he comes back, please, to call at our house as soon as he can."

Tryon was in that state of somnolence in which one may dream and yet be aware that one is dreaming,—the state where one, during a dream, dreams that one pinches one's self to be sure that one is not dreaming. He was therefore aware of a ringing quality about the words he had just heard that did not comport with the shadowy converse of a dream—an incongruity in the remark, too, which marred the harmony of the vision. The shock was sufficient to disturb Tryon's slumber, and he struggled slowly back to consciousness. When fully awake, he thought he heard a light footfall descending the stairs.

"Was there some one here?" he inquired of the attendant in the outer office, who was visible through the open door.

"Yas, suh," replied the boy, "a young cullud 'oman wuz in jes' now, axin' fer de doctuh."

Tryon felt a momentary touch of annoyance that a negro woman should have intruded herself into his dream at its most interesting point. Nevertheless, the voice had been so real, his imagination had reproduced with such exactness the dulcet tones so dear to him, that he turned his head involuntarily and looked out of the window. He could just see the flutter of a woman's skirt disappearing around the corner.

A moment later the doctor came bustling in,—a plump, rosy man of fifty or more, with a frank, open countenance and an air of genial good nature. Such a doctor, Tryon fancied, ought to enjoy a wide popularity. His mere presence would suggest life and hope and healthfulness.

"My dear boy," exclaimed the doctor cordially, after Tryon had introduced himself, "I 'm delighted to meet you—or any one of the old blood. Your mother and I were sweethearts, long ago, when we both wore pinafores, and went to see our grandfather at Christmas; and I met her more than once, and paid her more than one compliment, after she had grown to be a fine young woman. You 're like her, too, but not quite so handsome—you've more of what I suppose to be the Tryon favor, though I never met your father. So one of old Duncan McSwayne's notes went so far as that? Well, well, I don't know where you won't find them. One of them turned up here the other day from New York.

"The man you want to see," he added later in the conversation, "is old Judge Straight. He 's getting somewhat stiff in the joints, but he knows more law, and more about the McSwayne estate, than any other two lawyers in town. If anybody can collect your claim, Judge Straight can. I 'll send my boy Dave over to his office. Dave," he called to his attendant, "run over to Judge Straight's office and see if he 's there.

"There was a freshet here a few weeks ago," he went on, when the colored man had departed, "and they had to open the flood-gates and let the water out of the mill pond, for if the dam had broken, as it did twenty years ago, it would have washed the pillars from under the judge's office and let it down in the creek, and"—

"Jedge Straight ain't in de office jes' now, suh," reported the doctor's man Dave, from the head of the stairs.

"Did you ask when he'd be back?"

"No, suh, you did n't tell me ter, suh."

"Well, now, go back and inquire."

"The niggers," he explained to Tryon, "are getting mighty trifling since they've been freed. Before the war, that boy would have been around there and back before you could say Jack Robinson; now, the lazy rascal takes his time just like a white man."

Dave returned more promptly than from his first trip.

90

"Jedge Straight's dere now, suh," he said. "He 's done come in."

"I'll take you right around and introduce you," said the doctor, running on pleasantly, like a babbling brook. "I don't know whether the judge ever met your mother or not, but he knows a gentleman when he sees one, and will be glad to meet you and look after your affair. See to the patients, Dave, and say I'll be back shortly, and don't forget any messages left for me. Look sharp, now! You know your failing!"

They found Judge Straight in his office. He was seated by the rear window, and had fallen into a gentle doze—the air of Patesville was conducive to slumber. A visitor from some bustling city might have rubbed his eyes, on any but a market-day, and imagined the whole town asleep—that the people were somnambulists and did not know it. The judge, an old hand, roused himself so skillfully, at the sound of approaching footsteps, that his visitors could not guess but that he had been wide awake. He shook hands with the doctor, and acknowledged the introduction to Tryon with a rare old-fashioned courtesy, which the young man thought a very charming survival of the manners of a past and happier age.

"No," replied the judge, in answer to a question by Dr. Green, "I never met his mother; I was a generation ahead of her. I was at school with her father, however, fifty years ago—fifty years ago! No doubt that seems to you a long time, young gentleman?"

"It is a long time, sir," replied Tryon. "I must live more than twice as long as I have in order to cover it."

"A long time, and a troubled time," sighed the judge. "I could wish that I might see this unhappy land at peace with itself before I die. Things are in a sad tangle; I can't see the way out. But the worst enemy has been slain, in spite of us. We are well rid of slavery."

"But the negro we still have with us," remarked the doctor, "for here comes my man Dave. What is it, Dave?" he asked sharply, as the negro stuck his head in at the door.

"Doctuh Green," he said, "I fuhgot ter tell you, suh, dat dat young 'oman wuz at de office agin jes' befo' you come in, an' said fer you to go right down an' see her mammy ez soon ez you could."

"Ah, yes, and you 've just remembered it! I 'm afraid you 're entirely too forgetful for a doctor's office. You forgot about old Mrs. Latimer, the other day, and when I got there she had almost choked to death. Now get back to the office, and remember, the next time you forget anything, I'll hire another boy; remember that! That boy's head," he remarked to his companions, after Dave had gone, "reminds me of nothing so much as a dried gourd, with a handful of cowpeas rattling around it, in lieu of gray matter. An old woman out in Redbank got a fishbone in her throat, the other day, and nearly choked to death before I got there. A white woman, sir, came very near losing her life because of a lazy, trifling negro!"

"I should think you would discharge him, sir," suggested Tryon.

"What would be the use?" rejoined the doctor. "All negroes are alike, except that now and then there 's a pretty woman along the border-line. Take this patient of mine, for instance,—I 'll call on her after dinner, her case is not serious,—thirty years ago she would have made any man turn his head to look at her. You know who I mean, don't you, judge?"

92

"Yes. I think so," said the judge promptly. "I 've transacted a little business for her now and then."

"I don't know whether you've seen the daughter or not—I 'm sure you have n't for the past year or so, for she 's been away. But she 's in town now, and, by Jove, the girl is really beautiful. And I 'm a judge of beauty. Do you remember my wife thirty years ago, judge?"

"She was a very handsome woman, Ed," replied the other judicially. "If I had been twenty years younger, I should have cut you out."

"You mean you would have tried. But as I was saying, this girl is a beauty; I reckon we might guess where she got some of it, eh, Judge? Human nature is human nature, but it 's a d—d shame that a man should beget a child like that and leave it to live the life open for a negro. If she had been born white, the young fellows would be tumbling over one another to get her. Her mother would have to look after her pretty closely as things are, if she stayed here; but she disappeared mysteriously a year or two ago, and has been at the North, I 'm told, passing for white. She 'll probably marry a Yankee; he won't know any better, and it will serve him right—she 's only too white for them. She has a very striking figure, something on the Greek order, stately and slow-moving. She has the manners of a lady, too—a beautiful woman, if she is a nigger!"

"I quite agree with you, Ed," remarked the judge dryly, "that the mother had better look closely after the daughter."

"Ah, no, judge," replied the other, with a flattered smile, "my admiration for beauty is purely abstract. Twenty-five years ago, when I was younger"—

"When you were young," corrected the judge.

"When you and I were younger," continued the doctor ingeniously,—"twenty-five years ago, I could not have answered for myself. But I would advise the girl to stay at the North, if she can. She 's certainly out of place around here."

Tryon found the subject a little tiresome, and the doctor's enthusiasm not at all contagious. He could not possibly have been interested in a colored girl, under any circumstances, and he was engaged to be married to the most beautiful white woman on earth. To mention a negro woman in the same room where he was thinking of Rena seemed little short of profanation. His friend the doctor was a jovial fellow, but it was surely doubtful taste to refer to his wife in such a conversation. He was very glad when the doctor dropped the subject and permitted him to go more into detail about the matter which formed his business in Patesville. He took out of his pocket the papers concerning the McSwayne claim and laid them on the judge's desk.

"You 'll find everything there, sir,—the note, the contract, and some correspondence that will give you the hang of the thing. Will you be able to look over them to-day? I should like," he added a little nervously, "to go back to-morrow."

"What!" exclaimed Dr. Green vivaciously, "insult our town by staying only one day? It won't be long enough to get acquainted with our young ladies. Patesville girls are famous for their beauty. But perhaps there's a loadstone in South Carolina to draw you back? Ah, you change color! To my mind there's nothing finer than the ingenuous blush of youth. But we 'll spare you if you 'll answer one question—is it serious?"

"I'm to be married in two weeks, sir," answered Tryon. The statement sounded very pleasant, in spite of the slight embarrassment caused by the inquiry.

"Good boy!" rejoined the doctor, taking his arm familiarly—they were both standing now. "You ought to have married a Patesville girl, but you people down towards the eastern counties seldom come this way, and we are evidently too late to catch you."

"I'll look your papers over this morning," said the judge, "and when I come from dinner will stop at the court house and examine the records and see whether there's anything we can get hold of. If you'll drop in around three or four o'clock, I may be able to give you an opinion."

"Now, George," exclaimed the, doctor, "we'll go back to the office for a spell, and then I'll take you home with me to luncheon."

Tryon hesitated.

"Oh, you must come! Mrs. Green would never forgive me if I did n't bring you. Strangers are rare birds in our society, and when they come we make them welcome. Our enemies may overturn our institutions, and try to put the bottom rail on top, but they cannot destroy our Southern hospitality. There are so many carpet-baggers and other social vermin creeping into the South, with the Yankees trying to force the niggers on us, that it's a genuine pleasure to get acquainted with another real Southern gentleman, whom one can invite into one's house without fear of contamination, and before whom one can express his feelings freely and be sure of perfect sympathy."

XIII
AN INJUDICIOUS PAYMENT

WHEN Judge Straight's visitors had departed, he took up the papers which had been laid loosely on the table as they were taken out of Tryon's breast-pocket, and commenced their perusal. There was a note for five hundred dollars, many years overdue, but not yet outlawed by lapse of time; a contract covering the transaction out of which the note had grown; and several letters and copies of letters modifying the terms of the contract. The judge had glanced over most of the papers, and was getting well into the merits of the case, when he unfolded a letter which read as follows:—

MY DEAREST GEORGE,—I am going away for about a week, to visit the bedside of an old friend, who is very ill, and may not live. Do not be alarmed about me, for I shall very likely be back by the time you are.

Yours lovingly,
ROWENA WARWICK.

The judge was unable to connect this letter with the transaction which formed the subject of his examination. Age had dimmed his perceptions somewhat, and it was not until he had finished the letter, and read it over again, and noted the signature at the bottom a second time, that he perceived that the writing was in a woman's hand, that the ink was comparatively fresh, and that the letter was dated only a couple of days before. While he still held the sheet in his hand, it dawned upon him slowly that he held also one of the links in a chain of possible tragedy which he himself, he became uncomfortably aware, had had a hand in forging.

"It is the Walden woman's daughter, as sure as fate! Her name is Rena. Her brother goes by the name of Warwick. She has come to visit her sick mother. My young client, Green's relation, is her lover—is engaged to marry her—is in town, and is likely to meet her!"

The judge was so absorbed in the situation thus suggested that he laid the papers down and pondered for a moment the curious problem involved. He was quite aware that two races had not dwelt together, side by side, for nearly three hundred years, without mingling their blood in greater or less degree; he was old enough, and had seen curious things enough, to know that in this mingling the current had not always flowed in one direction. Certain old decisions with which he was familiar; old scandals that had crept along obscure channels; old facts that had come to the knowledge of an old practitioner, who held in the hollow of his hand the honor of more than one family, made him know that there was dark blood among the white people—not a great deal, and that very much diluted, and, so long as it was sedulously concealed or vigorously denied, or lost in the mists of tradition, or ascribed to a foreign or an aboriginal strain, having no perceptible effect upon the racial type.

Such people were, for the most part, merely on the ragged edge of the white world, seldom rising above the level of overseers, or slave-catchers, or sheriff's officers, who could usually be relied upon to resent the drop of black blood that tainted them, and with the zeal of the proselyte to visit their hatred of it upon the unfortunate blacks that fell into their hands. One curse of negro slavery was, and one part of its baleful heritage is, that it poisoned the fountains of human sympathy. Under a system where men might sell their own children without social reprobation or loss of prestige, it was not surprising that some of them should hate their distant cousins. There were not in Patesville half a dozen persons capable of thinking Judge Straight's thoughts upon the question before him, and perhaps not another who would have adopted the course he now pursued toward this anomalous family in the house behind the cedars.

"Well, here we are again, as the clown in the circus remarks," murmured the judge. "Ten years ago, in a moment of sentimental weakness and of quixotic loyalty to the memory of an old friend,—who, by the way, had not cared enough for his own children to take them away from the South, as he might have done, or to provide for them handsomely, as he perhaps meant to do,—I violated the traditions of my class and stepped from the beaten path to help the misbegotten son of my old friend out of the slough of despond, in which he had learned, in some strange way, that he was floundering. Ten years later, the ghost of my good deed returns to haunt me, and makes me doubt whether I have wrought more evil than good. I wonder," he mused, "if he will find her out?"

The judge was a man of imagination; he had read many books and had personally outlived some prejudices. He let his mind run on the various phases of the situation.

"If he found her out, would he by any possibility marry her?"

"It is not likely," he answered himself. "If he made the discovery here, the facts would probably leak out in the town. It is something that a man might do in secret, but only a hero or a fool would do openly."

The judge sighed as he contemplated another possibility. He had lived for seventy years under the old régime. The young man was a gentleman—so had been the girl's father. Conditions were changed, but human nature was the same. Would the young man's love turn to disgust and repulsion, or would it merely sink from the level of worship to that of desire? Would the girl, denied marriage, accept anything less? Her mother had,—but conditions were changed. Yes, conditions were changed, so far as the girl was concerned; there was a possible future for her under the new order of things; but white people had not changed their opinion of the negroes, except for the worse. The general belief was that they were just as inferior as before, and had, moreover, been spoiled by a disgusting assumption of equality, driven into their thick skulls by Yankee malignity bent upon humiliating a proud though vanquished foe.

If the judge had had sons and daughters of his own, he might not have done what he now proceeded to do. But the old man's attitude toward society was chiefly that of an observer, and the narrow stream of sentiment left in his heart chose to flow toward the weaker party in this unequal conflict,—a young woman fighting for love and opportunity against the ranked forces of society, against immemorial tradition, against pride of family and of race.

"It may be the unwisest thing I ever did," he said to himself, turning to his desk and taking up a quill pen, "and may result in more harm than good; but I was always from childhood in sympathy with the under dog. There is certainly as much reason in my helping the girl as the boy, for being a woman, she is less able to help herself."

He dipped his pen into the ink and wrote the following lines:—

MADAM,—If you value your daughter's happiness, keep her at home for the next day or two.

This note he dried by sprinkling it with sand from a box near at hand, signed with his own name, and, with a fine courtesy, addressed to "Mrs. Molly Walden." Having first carefully sealed it in an envelope, he stepped to the open door, and spied, playing marbles on the street near by, a group of negro boys, one of whom the judge called by name.

"Here, Billy," he said, handing the boy the note, "take this to Mis' Molly Walden. Do you know where she lives—down on Front Street, in the house behind the cedars?"

"Yas, suh, I knows de place."

"Make haste, now. When you come back and tell me what she says, I'll give you ten cents. On second thoughts, I shall be gone to lunch, so here's your money," he added, handing the lad the bit of soiled paper by which the United States government acknowledged its indebtedness to the bearer in the sum of ten cents.

Just here, however, the judge made his mistake. Very few mortals can spare the spring of hope, the motive force of expectation. The boy kept the note in his hand, winked at his companions, who had gathered as near as their awe of the judge would permit, and started down the street. As soon as the judge had disappeared, Billy beckoned to his friends, who speedily overtook him. When the party turned the corner of Front Street and were safely out of sight of Judge Straight's office, the capitalist entered the grocery store and invested his un-earned increment in gingerbread. When the ensuing saturnalia was over, Billy finished the game of marbles which the judge had interrupted, and then set out to ex-ecute his commission. He had nearly reached his objec-tive point when he met upon the street a young white lady, whom he did not know, and for whom, the path be-ing narrow at that point, he stepped out into the gutter. He reached the house behind the cedars, went round to the back door, and handed the envelope to Mis' Molly, who was seated on the rear piazza, propped up by pil-lows in a comfortable rocking-chair.

"Laws-a-massy!" she exclaimed weakly, "what is it?"

"It's a lettuh, ma'm," answered the boy, whose expand-ing nostrils had caught a pleasant odor from the kitchen, and who was therefore in no hurry to go away.

"Who 's it fur?" she asked.

"It's fuh you, ma'm," replied the lad.

"An' who's it from?" she inquired, turning the enve-lope over and over, and examining it with the impotent curiosity of one who cannot read.

"F'm ole Jedge Straight, ma'm. He tole me ter fetch it ter you. Is you got a roasted 'tater you could gimme, ma'm?"

"Shorely, chile. I 'll have Aunt Zilphy fetch you a piece of 'tater pone, if you'll hol' on a minute."

She called to Aunt Zilphy, who soon came hobbling out of the kitchen with a large square of the delicacy,— a flat cake made of mashed sweet potatoes, mixed with beaten eggs, sweetened and flavored to suit the taste, and baked in a Dutch oven upon the open hearth.

The boy took the gratuity, thanked her, and turned to go. Mis' Molly was still scanning the superscription of the letter. "I wonder," she murmured, "what old Judge Straight can be writin' to me about. Oh, boy!"

"Yas'm," answered the messenger, looking back.

"Can you read writin'?"

"No 'm."

"All right. Never mind."

She laid the letter carefully on the chimney-piece of the kitchen. "I reckon it's somethin' mo' 'bout the taxes," she thought, "or maybe somebody wants to buy one er my lots. Rena 'll be back terreckly, an' she kin read it an' find out. I'm glad my child'en have be'n to school. They never could have got where they are now if they had n't."

XIV
A LOYAL FRIEND

MENTION has been made of certain addressed envelopes which John Warwick, on the occasion of his visit to Patesville, had left with his illiterate mother, by the use of which she might communicate with her children from time to time. On one occasion, Mis' Molly, having had a letter written, took one of these envelopes from the chest where she kept her most valued possessions, and was about to inclose the letter when some one knocked at the back door. She laid the envelope and letter on a table in her bedroom, and went to answer the knock. The wind, blowing across the room through the open windows, picked up the envelope and bore it into the street. Mis' Molly, on her return, missed it, looked for it, and being unable to find it, took another envelope. An hour or two later another gust of wind lifted the bit of paper from the ground and carried it into the open door of the cooper shop. Frank picked it up, and observing that it was clean and unused, read the superscription. In his conversations with Mis' Molly, which were often about Rena,—the subject uppermost in both their minds,—he had noted the mystery maintained by Mis' Molly about her daughter's whereabouts, and had often wondered where she might be. Frank was an intelligent fellow, and could put this and that together. The envelope was addressed to a place in South Carolina. He was aware, from some casual remark of Mis' Molly's, that Rena had gone to live in South Carolina. Her son's name was John—that he had changed his last name was more than likely. Frank was not long in reaching the conclusion that Rena was to be found near the town named on the envelope, which he carefully preserved for future reference.

For a whole year Frank had yearned for a smile or a kind word from the only woman in the world. Peter, his father, had rallied him somewhat upon his moodiness after Rena's departure.

"Now 's de time, boy, fer you ter be lookin' roun' fer some nice gal er yo' own color, w'at'll 'preciate you, an' won't be 'shamed er you. You're wastin' time, boy, wastin' time, shootin' at a mark outer yo' range."

But Frank said nothing in reply, and afterwards the old man, who was not without discernment, respected his son's mood and was silent in turn; while Frank fed his memory with his imagination, and by their joint aid kept hope alive.

Later an opportunity to see her presented itself. Business in the cooper shop was dull. A barrel factory had been opened in the town, and had well-nigh paralyzed the cooper's trade. The best mechanic could hardly compete with a machine. One man could now easily do the work of Peter's shop. An agent appeared in town seeking laborers for one of the railroads which the newly organized carpet-bag governments were promoting. Upon inquiry Frank learned that their destination was near the town of Clarence, South Carolina. He promptly engaged himself for the service, and was soon at work in the neighborhood of Warwick's home. There he was employed steadily until a certain holiday, upon which a grand tournament was advertised to take place in a neighboring town. Work was suspended, and foremen and laborers attended the festivities.

Frank had surmised that Rena would be present on such an occasion. He had more than guessed, too, that she must be looked for among the white people rather than among the black. Hence the interest with which he had scanned the grand stand. The result has already been recounted. He had recognized her sweet face; he had seen her enthroned among the proudest and best. He had witnessed and gloried in her triumph. He had seen her cheek flushed with pleasure, her eyes lit up with smiles. He had followed her carriage, had made the acquaintance of Mimy the nurse, and had learned all about the family. When finally he left the neighborhood to return to Patesville, he had learned of Tryon's attentions, and had heard the servants' gossip with reference to the marriage, of which they knew the details long before the principals had approached the main fact. Frank went away without having received one smile or heard one word from Rena; but he had seen her: she was happy; he was content in the knowledge of her happiness. She was doubtless secure in the belief that her secret was unknown. Why should he, by revealing his presence, sow the seeds of doubt or distrust in the garden of her happiness? He sacrificed the deepest longing of a faithful heart, and went back to the cooper shop lest perchance she might accidentally come upon him some day and suffer the shock which he had sedulously spared her.

"I would n' want ter skeer her," he mused, "er make her feel bad, an' dat 's w'at I 'd mos' lackly do ef she seed me. She 'll be better off wid me out'n de road. She 'll marry dat rich w'ite gent'eman,—he won't never know de diffe'nce,—an' be a w'ite lady, ez she would 'a' be'n, ef some ole witch had n' changed her in her cradle. But maybe some time she 'll 'member de little nigger w'at use' ter nuss her w'en she wuz a chile, an' fished her out'n de ole canal, an' would 'a' died fer her ef it would 'a' done any good."

Very generously too, and with a fine delicacy, he said nothing to Mis' Molly of his having seen her daughter, lest she might be disquieted by the knowledge that he shared the family secret,—no great mystery now, this pitiful secret, but more far-reaching in its consequences than any blood-curdling crime. The taint of black blood was the unpardonable sin, from the unmerited penalty of which there was no escape except by concealment. If there be a dainty reader of this tale who scorns a lie, and who writes the story of his life upon his sleeve for all the world to read, let him uncurl his scornful lip and come down from the pedestal of superior morality, to which assured position and wide opportunity have lifted him, and put himself in the place of Rena and her brother, upon whom God had lavished his best gifts, and from whom society would have withheld all that made these gifts valuable. To undertake what they tried to do required great courage. Had they possessed the sneaking, cringing, treacherous character traditionally ascribed to people of mixed blood—the character which the blessed institutions of a free slave-holding republic had been well adapted to foster among them; had they been selfish enough to sacrifice to their ambition the mother who gave them birth, society would have been placated or humbugged, and the voyage of their life might have been one of unbroken smoothness.

When Rena came back unexpectedly at the behest of her dream, Frank heard again the music of her voice, felt the joy of her presence and the benison of her smile. There was, however, a subtle difference in her bearing. Her words were not less kind, but they seemed to come from a remoter source. She was kind, as the sun is warm or the rain refreshing; she was especially kind to Frank, because he had been good to her mother. If Frank felt the difference in her attitude, he ascribed it to the fact that she had been white, and had taken on something of the white attitude toward the negro; and Frank, with an equal unconsciousness, clothed her with the attributes of the superior race. Only her drop of black blood, he conceived, gave him the right to feel toward her as he would never have felt without it; and if Rena guessed her faithful devotee's secret, the same reason saved his worship from presumption. A smile and a kind word were little enough to pay for a life's devotion.

On the third day of Rena's presence in Patesville, Frank was driving up Front Street in the early afternoon, when he nearly fell off his cart in astonishment as he saw seated in Dr. Green's buggy, which was standing in front of the Patesville Hotel, the young gentleman who had won the prize at the tournament, and who, as he had learned, was to marry Rena. Frank was quite certain that she did not know of Tryon's presence in the town. Frank had been over to Mis' Molly's in the morning, and had offered his services to the sick woman, who had rapidly become convalescent upon her daughter's return. Mis' Molly had spoken of some camphor that she needed. Frank had volunteered to get it. Rena had thanked him, and had spoken of going to the drugstore during the afternoon. It was her intention to leave Patesville on the following day.

"Ef dat man sees her in dis town," said Frank to himself, "dere 'll be trouble. She don't know *he 's* here, an' I 'll bet he don't know *she 's* here."

Then Frank was assailed by a very strong temptation. If, as he surmised, the joint presence of the two lovers in Patesville was a mere coincidence, a meeting between them would probably result in the discovery of Rena's secret.

"If she 's found out," argued the tempter, "she 'll come back to her mother, and you can see her every day."

But Frank's love was not of the selfish kind. He put temptation aside, and applied the whip to the back of his mule with a vigor that astonished the animal and moved him to unwonted activity. In an unusually short space of time he drew up before Mis' Molly's back gate, sprang from the cart, and ran up to Mis' Molly on the porch.

"Is Miss Rena here?" he demanded breathlessly.

"No, Frank; she went up town 'bout an hour ago to see the doctor an' git me some camphor gum."

Frank uttered a groan, rushed from the house, sprang into the cart, and goaded the terrified mule into a gallop that carried him back to the market-house in half the time it had taken him to reach Mis' Molly's.

"I wonder what in the worl' 's the matter with Frank," mused Mis' Molly, in vague alarm. "Ef he had n't be'n in such a hurry, I'd 'a' axed him to read Judge Straight's letter. But Rena 'll be home soon."

When Frank reached the doctor's office, he saw Tryon seated in the doctor's buggy, which was standing by the window of the drugstore. Frank ran upstairs and asked the doctor's man if Miss Walden had been there.

"Yas," replied Dave, "she wuz here a little w'ile ago, an' said she wuz gwine downstairs ter de drugsto'. I would n' be s'prise' ef you'd fin' her dere now."

XV

MINE OWN PEOPLE

THE drive by which Dr. Green took Tryon to his own house led up Front Street about a mile, to the most aristocratic portion of the town, situated on the hill known as Haymount, or, more briefly, "The Hill." The Hill had lost some of its former glory, however, for the blight of a four years' war was everywhere. After reaching the top of this wooded eminence, the road skirted for some little distance the brow of the hill. Below them lay the picturesque old town, a mass of vivid green, dotted here and there with gray roofs that rose above the tree-tops. Two long ribbons of streets stretched away from the Hill to the faint red line that marked the high bluff beyond the river at the farther side of the town. The market-house tower and the slender spires of half a dozen churches were sharply outlined against the green background. The face of the clock was visible, but the hours could have been read only by eyes of phenomenal sharpness. Around them stretched ruined walls, dismantled towers, and crumbling earthworks—footprints of the god of war, one of whose temples had crowned this height. For many years before the rebellion a Federal arsenal had been located at Patesville. Seized by the state troops upon the secession of North Carolina, it had been held by the Confederates until the approach of Sherman's victorious army, whereupon it was evacuated and partially destroyed. The work of destruction begun by the retreating garrison was completed by the conquerors, and now only ruined walls and broken cannon remained of what had once been the chief ornament and pride of Patesville.

The front of Dr. Green's spacious brick house, which occupied an ideally picturesque site, was overgrown by a network of clinging vines, contrasting most agreeably with the mellow red background. A low brick wall, also overrun with creepers, separated the premises from the street and shut in a well-kept flower garden, in which

Tryon, who knew something of plants, noticed many rare and beautiful specimens.

Mrs. Green greeted Tryon cordially. He did not have the doctor's memory with which to fill out the lady's cheeks or restore the lustre of her hair or the sparkle of her eyes, and thereby justify her husband's claim to be a judge of beauty; but her kind-hearted hospitality was obvious, and might have made even a plain woman seem handsome. She and her two fair daughters, to whom Tryon was duly presented, looked with much favor upon their handsome young kinsman; for among the people of Patesville, perhaps by virtue of the prevalence of Scottish blood, the ties of blood were cherished as things of value, and never forgotten except in case of the unworthy—an exception, by the way, which one need hardly go so far to seek.

The Patesville people were not exceptional in the weaknesses and meannesses which are common to all mankind, but for some of the finer social qualities they were conspicuously above the average. Kindness, hospitality, loyalty, a chivalrous deference to women,—all these things might be found in large measure by those who saw Patesville with the eyes of its best citizens, and accepted their standards of politics, religion, manners, and morals.

The doctor, after the introductions, excused himself for a moment. Mrs. Green soon left Tryon with the young ladies and went to look after luncheon. Her first errand, however, was to find the doctor.

"Is he well off, Ed?" she asked her husband.

"Lots of land, and plenty of money, if he is ever able to collect it. He has inherited two estates."

"He's a good-looking fellow," she mused. "Is he married?"

"There you go again," replied her husband, shaking his forefinger at her in mock reproach. "To a woman with marriageable daughters all roads lead to matrimony, the centre of a woman's universe. All men must be sized up by their matrimonial availability. No, he is n't married."

"That's nice," she rejoined reflectively. "I think we ought to ask him to stay with us while he is in town, don't you?"

"He's not married," rejoined the doctor slyly, "but the next best thing—he's engaged."

"Come to think of it," said the lady, "I'm afraid we would n't have the room to spare, and the girls would hardly have time to entertain him. But we 'll have him up several times. I like his looks. I wish you had sent me word he was coming; I 'd have had a better luncheon."

"Make him a salad," rejoined the doctor, "and get out a bottle of the best claret. Thank God, the Yankees did n't get into my wine cellar! The young man must be treated with genuine Southern hospitality,—even if he were a Mormon and married ten times over."

"Indeed, he would not, Ed,—the idea! I 'm ashamed of you. Hurry back to the parlor and talk to him. The girls may want to primp a little before luncheon; we don't have a young man every day."

"Beauty unadorned," replied the doctor, "is adorned the most. My profession qualifies me to speak upon the subject. They are the two handsomest young women in Patesville, and the daughters of the most beautiful"—

"Don't you dare to say the word," interrupted Mrs. Green, with placid good nature. "I shall never grow old

111

while I am living with a big boy like you. But I must go and make the salad."

At dinner the conversation ran on the family connections and their varying fortunes in the late war. Some had died upon the battlefield, and slept in unknown graves; some had been financially ruined by their faith in the "lost cause," having invested their all in the securities of the Confederate Government. Few had anything left but land, and land without slaves to work it was a drug in the market.

"I was offered a thousand acres, the other day, at twenty-five cents an acre," remarked the doctor. "The owner is so land-poor that he can't pay the taxes. They have taken our negroes and our liberties. It may be better for our grandchildren that the negroes are free, but it's confoundedly hard on us to take them without paying for them. They may exalt our slaves over us temporarily, but they have not broken our spirit, and cannot take away our superiority of blood and breeding. In time we shall regain control. The negro is an inferior creature; God has marked him with the badge of servitude, and has adjusted his intellect to a servile condition. We will not long submit to his domination. I give you a toast, sir: The Anglo-Saxon race: may it remain forever, as now, the head and front of creation, never yielding its rights, and ready always to die, if need be, in defense of its liberties!"

"With all my heart, sir," replied Tryon, who felt in this company a thrill of that pleasure which accompanies conscious superiority,—"with all my heart, sir, if the ladies will permit me."

"We will join you," they replied. The toast was drunk with great enthusiasm.

"And now, my dear George," exclaimed the doctor, "to change one good subject for another, tell us who is the favored lady?"

"A Miss Rowena Warwick, sir," replied Tryon, vividly conscious of four pairs of eyes fixed upon him, but, apart from the momentary embarrassment, welcoming the subject as the one he would most like to speak upon.

"A good, strong old English name," observed the doctor.

"The heroine of 'Ivanhoe'!" exclaimed Miss Harriet.

"Warwick the Kingmaker!" said Miss Mary. "Is she tall and fair, and dignified and stately?"

"She is tall, dark rather than fair, and full of tender grace and sweet humility."

"She should have been named Rebecca instead of Rowena," rejoined Miss Mary, who was well up in her Scott.

"Tell us something about her people," asked Mrs. Green,—to which inquiry the young ladies looked assent.

In this meeting of the elect of his own class and kin Warwick felt a certain strong illumination upon the value of birth and blood. Finding Rena among people of the best social standing, the subsequent intimation that she was a girl of no family had seemed a small matter to one so much in love. Nevertheless, in his present company he felt a decided satisfaction in being able to present for his future wife a clean bill of social health.

"Her brother is the most prominent lawyer of Clarence. They live in a fine old family mansion, and are among the best people of the town."

"Quite right, my boy," assented the doctor. "None but the best are good enough for the best. You must bring her to Patesville some day. But bless my life!" he exclaimed, looking at his watch, "I must be going. Will you stay with the ladies awhile, or go back down town with me?"

"I think I had better go with you, sir. I shall have to see Judge Straight."

"Very well. But you must come back to supper, and we'll have a few friends in to meet you. You must see some of the best people."

The doctor's buggy was waiting at the gate. As they were passing the hotel on their drive down town, the clerk came out to the curbstone and called to the doctor.

"There's a man here, doctor, who's been taken suddenly ill. Can you come in a minute?"

"I suppose I'll have to. Will you wait for me here, George, or will you drive down to the office? I can walk the rest of the way."

"I think I'll wait here, doctor," answered Tryon. "I'll step up to my room a moment. I'll be back by the time you're ready."

It was while they were standing before the hotel, before alighting from the buggy, that Frank Fowler, passing on his cart, saw Tryon and set out as fast as he could to warn Mis' Molly and her daughter of his presence in the town.

Tryon went up to his room, returned after a while, and resumed his seat in the buggy, where he waited fifteen minutes longer before the doctor was ready. When they drew up in front of the office, the doctor's man Dave was standing in the doorway, looking up the street with an anxious expression, as though struggling hard to keep something upon his mind.

"Anything wanted, Dave?" asked the doctor.

"Dat young 'oman's be'n heah ag'in, suh, an' wants ter see you bad. She's in de drugstore dere now, suh. Bless Gawd!" he added to himself fervently, "I 'membered dat. Dis yer recommemb'ance er mine is gwine ter git me inter trouble ef I don' look out, an' dat's a fac', sho'."

The doctor sprang from the buggy with an agility remarkable in a man of sixty. "Just keep your seat, George," he said to Tryon, "until I have spoken to the young woman, and then we'll go across to Straight's. Or, if you'll drive along a little farther, you can see the girl through the window. She 's worth the trouble, if you like a pretty face."

Tryon liked one pretty face; moreover, tinted beauty had never appealed to him. More to show a proper regard for what interested the doctor than from any curiosity of his own, he drove forward a few feet, until the side of the buggy was opposite the drugstore window, and then looked in.

Between the colored glass bottles in the window he could see a young woman, a tall and slender girl, like a lily on its stem. She stood talking with the doctor, who held his hat in his hand with as much deference as though she were the proudest dame in town. Her face was partly turned away from the window, but as Tryon's eye fell upon her, he gave a great start. Surely, no two women could be so much alike. The height, the graceful droop of the shoulders, the swan-like poise of the head, the well-turned little ear,—surely, no two women could have them all identical! But, pshaw! the notion was absurd, it was merely the reflex influence of his morning's dream.

She moved slightly; it was Rena's movement. Surely he knew the gown, and the style of hair-dressing! She rested her hand lightly on the back of a chair. The ring that glittered on her finger could be none other than his own.

The doctor bowed. The girl nodded in response, and, turning, left the store. Tryon leaned forward from the buggy-seat and kept his eye fixed on the figure that moved across the floor of the drugstore. As she came out, she turned her face casually toward the buggy, and there could no longer be any doubt as to her identity.

When Rena's eyes fell upon the young man in the buggy, she saw a face as pale as death, with starting eyes, in which love, which once had reigned there, had now given place to astonishment and horror. She stood a moment as if turned to stone. One appealing glance she gave,—a look that might have softened adamant. When she saw that it brought no answering sign of love or sorrow or regret, the color faded from her cheek, the light from her eye, and she fell fainting to the ground.

XVI
THE BOTTOM FALLS OUT

THE first effect of Tryon's discovery was, figuratively speaking, to knock the bottom out of things for him. It was much as if a boat on which he had been floating smoothly down the stream of pleasure had sunk suddenly and left him struggling in deep waters. The full realization of the truth, which followed speedily, had for the moment reversed his mental attitude toward her, and love and yearning had given place to anger and disgust. His agitation could hardly have escaped notice had not the doctor's attention, and that of the crowd that quickly gathered, been absorbed by the young woman who had fallen. During the time occupied in carrying her into the drugstore, restoring her to consciousness, and sending her home in a carriage, Tryon had time to recover in some degree his self-possession. When Rena had been taken home, he slipped away for a long walk, after which he called at Judge Straight's office and received the judge's report upon the matter presented. Judge Straight had found the claim, in his opinion, a good one; he had discovered property from which, in case the claim were allowed, the amount might be realized. The judge, who had already been informed of the incident at the drugstore, observed Tryon's preoccupation and guessed shrewdly at its cause, but gave no sign. Tryon left the matter of the note unreservedly in the lawyer's hands, with instructions to communicate to him any further developments.

Returning to the doctor's office, Tryon listened to that genial gentleman's comments on the accident, his own concern in which he, by a great effort, was able to conceal. The doctor insisted upon his returning to the Hill for supper. Tryon pleaded illness. The doctor was solicitous, felt his pulse, examined his tongue, pronounced him feverish, and prescribed a sedative. Tryon sought refuge in his room at the hotel, from which he did not emerge again until morning.

His emotions were varied and stormy. At first he could

see nothing but the fraud of which he had been made the victim. A negro girl had been foisted upon him for a white woman, and he had almost committed the unpardonable sin against his race of marrying her. Such a step, he felt, would have been criminal at any time; it would have been the most odious treachery at this epoch, when his people had been subjugated and humiliated by the Northern invaders, who had preached negro equality and abolished the wholesome laws decreeing the separation of the races. But no Southerner who loved his poor, downtrodden country, or his race, the proud Anglo-Saxon race which traced the clear stream of its blood to the cavaliers of England, could tolerate the idea that even in distant generations that unsullied current could be polluted by the blood of slaves. The very thought was an insult to the white people of the South. For Tryon's liberality, of which he had spoken so nobly and so sincerely, had been confined unconsciously, and as a matter of course, within the boundaries of his own race. The Southern mind, in discussing abstract questions relative to humanity, makes always, consciously or unconsciously, the mental reservation that the conclusions reached do not apply to the negro, unless they can be made to harmonize with the customs of the country.

But reasoning thus was not without effect upon a mind by nature reasonable above the average. Tryon's race impulse and social prejudice had carried him too far, and the swing of the mental pendulum brought his thoughts rapidly back in the opposite direction. Tossing uneasily on the bed, where he had thrown himself down without undressing, the air of the room oppressed him, and he threw open the window. The cool night air calmed his throbbing pulses. The moonlight, streaming through the window, flooded the room with a soft light, in which he seemed to see Rena standing before him, as she had appeared that afternoon, gazing at him with eyes that implored charity and forgiveness. He burst into tears,—bitter tears, that strained his heartstrings. He was only a youth. She was his first love, and he had lost her forever. She was worse than dead to him; for if he had seen her lying in her shroud before him, he could at least have cherished her memory; now, even this consolation was denied him.

The town clock—which so long as it was wound up regularly recked nothing of love or hate, joy or sorrow—solemnly tolled out the hour of midnight and sounded the knell of his lost love. Lost she was, as though she had never been, as she had indeed had no right to be. He resolutely determined to banish her image from his mind. See her again he could not; it would be painful to them both; it could be productive of no good to either. He had felt the power and charm of love, and no ordinary shock could have loosened its hold; but this catastrophe, which had so rudely swept away the groundwork of his passion, had stirred into new life all the slumbering pride of race and ancestry which characterized his caste. How much of this sensitive superiority was essential and how much accidental; how much of it was due to the ever-suggested comparison with a servile race; how much of it was ignorance and self-conceit; to what extent the boasted purity of his race would have been contaminated by the fair woman whose image filled his memory,—of these things he never thought. He was not influenced by sordid considerations; he would have denied that his course was controlled by any narrow prudence. If Rena had been white, pure white (for in his creed there was no compromise), he would have braved any danger for her sake. Had she been merely of illegitimate birth, he would have overlooked the bar sinister. Had her people been simply poor and of low estate, he would have brushed aside mere worldly considerations, and would have bravely sacrificed convention for love; for his liberality was not a mere form of words. But the one objection which he could not overlook was, unhappily, the one that applied to the only woman who had as yet moved his heart. He tried to be angry with her, but after the first hour he found it impossible. He was a man of too much imagination not to be able to put himself, in some measure at least, in her place,—to perceive that for her the step which had placed her in Tryon's world was the working out of nature's great law of self-preservation, for which he could not blame her. But for the sheerest accident,— no, rather, but for a providential interference,—he would have married her, and might have gone to the grave unconscious that she was other than she seemed.

The clock struck the hour of two. With a shiver he closed the window, undressed by the moonlight, drew down the shade, and went to bed. He fell into an unquiet slumber, and dreamed again of Rena. He must learn to control his waking thoughts; his dreams could not be curbed. In that realm Rena's image was for many a day to remain supreme. He dreamed of her sweet smile, her soft touch, her gentle voice. In all her fair young beauty she stood before him, and then by some hellish magic she was slowly transformed into a hideous black hag. With agonized eyes he watched her beautiful tresses become mere wisps of coarse wool, wrapped round with dingy cotton strings; he saw her clear eyes grow bloodshot, her ivory teeth turn to unwholesome fangs. With a shudder he awoke, to find the cold gray dawn of a rainy day stealing through the window.

He rose, dressed himself, went down to breakfast, then entered the writing-room and penned a letter which, after reading it over, he tore into small pieces and threw into the waste-basket. A second shared the same fate. Giving up the task, he left the hotel and walked down to Dr. Green's office.

"Is the doctor in?" he asked of the colored attendant.

"No, suh," replied the man; "he 's gone ter see de young cullud gal w'at fainted w'en de doctuh was wid you yistiddy."

Tryon sat down at the doctor's desk and hastily scrawled a note, stating that business compelled his immediate departure. He thanked the doctor for courtesies extended, and left his regards for the ladies. Returning to the hotel, he paid his bill and took a hack for the wharf, from which a boat was due to leave at nine o'clock.

As the hack drove down Front Street, Tryon noted idly the houses that lined the street. When he reached the sordid district in the lower part of the town, there was nothing to attract his attention until the carriage came abreast of a row of cedar-trees, beyond which could be seen the upper part of a large house with dormer windows. Before the gate stood a horse and buggy, which Tryon thought he recognized as Dr. Green's. He leaned forward and addressed the driver.

"Can you tell me who lives there?" Tryon asked, pointing to the house.

"A cullud 'oman, suh," the man replied, touching his hat. "Mis' Molly Walden an' her daughter Rena."

The vivid impression he received of this house, and the spectre that rose before him of a pale, broken-hearted girl within its gray walls, weeping for a lost lover and a vanished dream of happiness, did not argue well for Tryon's future peace of mind. Rena's image was not to be easily expelled from his heart; for the laws of nature are higher and more potent than merely human institutions, and upon anything like a fair field are likely to win in the long run.

XVII
TWO LETTERS

WARWICK awaited events with some calmness and some philosophy,—he could hardly have had the one without the other; and it required much philosophy to make him wait a week in patience for information upon a subject in which he was so vitally interested. The delay pointed to disaster. Bad news being expected, delay at least put off the evil day. At the end of the week he received two letters,—one addressed in his own handwriting and post-marked Patesville, N. C.; the other in the handwriting of George Tryon. He opened the Patesville letter, which ran as follows:—

MY DEAR SON,—Frank is writing this letter for me. I am not well, but, thank the Lord, I am better than I was.

Rena has had a heap of trouble on account of me and my sickness. If I could of dreamt that I was going to do so much harm, I would of died and gone to meet my God without writing one word to spoil my girl's chances in life; but I did n't know what was going to happen, and I hope the Lord will forgive me.

Frank knows all about it, and so I am having him write this letter for me, as Rena is not well enough yet. Frank has been very good to me and to Rena. He was down to your place and saw Rena there, and never said a word about it to nobody, not even to me, because he did n't want to do Rena no harm. Frank is the best friend I have got in town, because he does so much for me and don't want nothing in return. (He tells me not to put this in about him, but I want you to know it.)

And now about Rena. She come to see me, and I got better right away, for it was longing for her as much as anything else that made me sick, and I was mighty mizzable. When she had been here three days and was going back next day, she went up town to see the doctor for me, and while she was up there she fainted and fell down in the street, and Dr. Green sent her home in his buggy and come down to see her. He could n't tell what was the matter with her, but she has been sick ever since and out of her head some of the time, and keeps on calling on somebody by the name of George, which was the young white man she told me she was going to marry. It seems he was in town the day Rena was took sick, for Frank saw him up street and run all the way down here to tell me, so that she could keep out of his way, while she was still up town waiting for the doctor and getting me some camphor gum for my camphor bottle. Old

Judge Straight must have knowed something about it, for he sent me a note to keep Rena in the house, but the little boy he sent it by did n't bring it till Rena was already gone up town, and, as I could n't read, of course I did n't know what it said. Dr. Green heard Rena running on while she was out of her head, and I reckon he must have suspicioned something, for he looked kind of queer and went away without saying nothing. Frank says she met this man on the street, and when he found out she was n't white, he said or done something that broke her heart and she fainted and fell down.

I am writing you this letter because I know you will be worrying about Rena not coming back. If it was n't for Frank, I hardly know how I could write to you. Frank is not going to say nothing about Rena's passing for white and meeting this man, and neither am I; and I don't suppose Judge Straight will say nothing, because he is our good friend; and Dr. Green won't say nothing about it, because Frank says Dr. Green's cook Nancy says this young man named George stopped with him and was some cousin or relation to the family, and they would n't want people to know that any of their kin was thinking about marrying a colored girl, and the white folks have all been mad since J. B. Thompson married his black housekeeper when she got religion and would n't live with him no more.

All the rest of the connection are well. I have just been in to see how Rena is. She is feeling some better, I think, and says give you her love and she will write you a letter in a few days, as soon as she is well enough. She bust out crying while she was talking, but I reckon that is better than being out of her head. I hope this may find you well, and that this man of Rena's won't say nor do nothing down there to hurt you. He has not wrote to Rena nor sent her no word. I reckon he is very mad.

Your affectionate mother,

MARY WALDEN.

This letter, while confirming Warwick's fears, relieved his suspense. He at least knew the worst, unless there should be something still more disturbing in Tryon's letter, which he now proceeded to open, and which ran as follows:—

JOHN WARWICK, ESQ.

Dear Sir,—When I inform you, as you are doubtless informed ere the receipt of this, that I saw your sister in Patesville last week and learned the nature of those antecedents of yours and hers at which you hinted so obscurely in a recent conversation, you will not be surprised to learn that I take this opportunity of renouncing any pretensions to Miss Warwick's hand, and request you to convey this message to her, since it was through you that I formed her acquaintance. I think perhaps that few white men would deem it necessary to make an explanation under the circumstances, and I do not know that I need say more than that no one, considering where and how I met your sister, would have dreamed of even the possibility of what I have learned. I might with justice reproach you for trifling with the most sacred feelings of a man's heart; but I realize the hardship of your position and hers, and can make allowances. I would never have sought to know this thing; I would doubtless have been happier had I gone through life without finding it

125

out; but having the knowledge, I cannot ignore it, as you must understand perfectly well. I regret that she should be distressed or disappointed,—she has not suffered alone.

I need scarcely assure you that I shall say nothing about this affair, and that I shall keep your secret as though it were my own. Personally, I shall never be able to think of you as other than a white man, as you may gather from the tone of this letter; and while I cannot marry your sister, I wish her every happiness, and remain,

Yours very truly,

GEORGE TRYON.

Warwick could not know that this formal epistle was the last of a dozen that Tryon had written and destroyed during the week since the meeting in Patesville,—hot, blistering letters, cold, cutting letters, scornful, crushing letters. Though none of them was sent, except this last, they had furnished a safety-valve for his emotions, and had left him in a state of mind that permitted him to write the foregoing.

And now, while Rena is recovering from her illness, and Tryon from his love, and while Fate is shuffling the cards for another deal, a few words may be said about the past life of the people who lived in the rear of the flower garden, in the quaint old house beyond the cedars, and how their lives were mingled with those of the men and women around them and others that were gone. For connected with our kind we must be; if not by our virtues, then by our vices,—if not by our services, at least by our needs.

XVIII
UNDER THE OLD REGIME

For many years before the civil war there had lived, in the old house behind the cedars, a free colored woman who went by the name of Molly Walden—her rightful name, for her parents were free-born and legally married. She was a tall woman, straight as an arrow. Her complexion in youth was of an old ivory tint, which at the period of this story, time had darkened measurably. Her black eyes, now faded, had once sparkled with the fire of youth. High cheek-bones, straight black hair, and a certain dignified reposefulness of manner pointed to an aboriginal descent. Tradition gave her to the negro race. Doubtless she had a strain of each, with white blood very visibly predominating over both. In Louisiana or the West Indies she would have been called a quadroon, or more loosely, a creole; in North Carolina, where fine distinctions were not the rule in matters of color, she was sufficiently differentiated when described as a bright mulatto.

Molly's free birth carried with it certain advantages, even in the South before the war. Though degraded from its high estate, and shorn of its choicest attributes, the word "freedom" had nevertheless a cheerful sound, and described a condition that left even to colored people who could claim it some liberty of movement and some control of their own persons. They were not citizens, yet they were not slaves. No negro, save in books, ever refused freedom; many of them ran frightful risks to achieve it. Molly's parents were of the class, more numerous in North Carolina than elsewhere, known as "old

issue free negroes," which took its rise in the misty colonial period, when race lines were not so closely drawn,
and the population of North Carolina comprised many
Indians, runaway negroes, and indentured white servants
from the seaboard plantations, who mingled their blood
with great freedom and small formality. Free colored
people in North Carolina exercised the right of suffrage
as late as 1835, and some of them, in spite of galling re-
strictions, attained to a considerable degree of prosperity, and dreamed of a still brighter future, when the growing tyranny of the slave power crushed their hopes and
crowded the free people back upon the black mass just
beneath them. Mis' Molly's father had been at one time
a man of some means. In an evil hour, with an overween-
ing confidence in his fellow men, he indorsed a note for
a white man who, in a moment of financial hardship,
clapped his colored neighbor on the back and called him
brother. Not poverty, but wealth, is the most potent leveler. In due time the indorser was called upon to meet
the maturing obligation. This was the beginning of a se-
ries of financial difficulties which speedily involved him
in ruin. He died prematurely, a disappointed and dis-
heartened man, leaving his family in dire poverty.

His widow and surviving children lived on for a little
while at the house he had owned, just outside of the
town, on one of the main traveled roads. By the wayside,
near the house, there was a famous deep well. The slim,
barefoot girl, with sparkling eyes and voluminous hair,
who played about the yard and sometimes handed water in a gourd to travelers, did not long escape critical
observation. A gentleman drove by one day, stopped at
the well, smiled upon the girl, and said kind words. He

came again, more than once, and soon, while scarcely more than a child in years, Molly was living in her own house, hers by deed of gift, for her protector was rich and liberal. Her mother nevermore knew want. Her poor relations could always find a meal in Molly's kitchen. She did not flaunt her prosperity in the world's face; she hid it discreetly behind the cedar screen. Those who wished could know of it, for there were few secrets in Patesville; those who chose could as easily ignore it. There were few to trouble themselves about the secluded life of an obscure woman of a class which had no recognized place in the social economy. She worshiped the ground upon which her lord walked, was humbly grateful for his protection, and quite as faithful as the forbidden marriage vow could possibly have made her. She led her life in material peace and comfort, and with a certain amount of dignity. Of her false relation to society she was not without some vague conception; but the moral point involved was so confused with other questions growing out of slavery and caste as to cause her, as a rule, but little uneasiness; and only now and then, in the moments of deeper feeling that come sometimes to all who live and love, did there break through the mists of ignorance and prejudice surrounding her a flash of light by which she saw, so far as she was capable of seeing, her true position, which in the clear light of truth no special pleading could entirely justify. For she was free, she had not the slave's excuse. With every inducement to do evil and few incentives to do well, and hence entitled to charitable judgment, she yet had freedom of choice, and therefore could not wholly escape blame. Let it be said, in further extenuation, that no other woman lived in neglect or sorrow because of her. She robbed no one else. For what life gave her she returned an equivalent; and what she did not pay, her children settled to the last farthing.

Several years before the war, when Mis' Molly's daughter Rena was a few years old, death had suddenly removed the source of their prosperity.

The household was not left entirely destitute. Mis' Molly owned her home, and had a store of gold pieces in the chest beneath her bed. A small piece of real estate stood in the name of each of the children, the income from which contributed to their maintenance. Larger expectations were dependent upon the discovery of a promised will, which never came to light. Mis' Molly wore black for several years after this bereavement, until the teacher and the preacher, following close upon the heels of military occupation, suggested to the colored people new standards of life and character, in the light of which Mis' Molly laid her mourning sadly and shamefacedly aside. She had eaten of the fruit of the Tree of Knowledge. After the war she formed the habit of church-going, and might have been seen now and then, with her daughter, in a retired corner of the gallery of the white Episcopal church. Upon the ground floor was a certain pew which could be seen from her seat, where once had sat a gentleman whose pleasures had not interfered with the practice of his religion. She might have had a better seat in a church where a Northern missionary would have preached a sermon better suited to her comprehension and her moral needs, but she preferred the other. She was not white, alas! she was shut out from this seeming paradise; but she liked to see the distant glow of the celestial city, and to recall the days when she had basked in its radiance. She did not sympathize greatly with the new era opened up for the emancipated slaves; she had no ideal love of liberty; she was no broader and no more altruistic than the white people around her, to whom she had always looked up; and she sighed for the old days, because to her they had been the good days. Now, not only was her king dead, but the shield of his memory protected her no longer.

Molly had lost one child, and his grave was visible from the kitchen window, under a small clump of cedars in the rear of the two-acre lot. For even in the towns many a household had its private cemetery in those old days when the living were close to the dead, and ghosts were not the mere chimeras of a sick imagination, but real though unsubstantial entities, of which it was almost disgraceful not to have seen one or two. Had not the Witch of Endor called up the shade of Samuel the prophet? Had not the spirit of Mis' Molly's dead son appeared to her, as well as the ghostly presence of another she had loved?

In 1855, Mis' Molly's remaining son had grown into a tall, slender lad of fifteen, with his father's patrician features and his mother's Indian hair, and no external sign to mark him off from the white boys on the street. He soon came to know, however, that there was a difference. He was informed one day that he was black. He denied the proposition and thrashed the child who made it. The scene was repeated the next day, with a variation,—he was himself thrashed by a larger boy. When he had been beaten five or six times, he ceased to argue the point, though to himself he never admitted the charge. His playmates might call him black; the mirror proved that

God, the Father of all, had made him white; and God, he had been taught, made no mistakes,—having made him white, He must have meant him to be white.

In the "hall" or parlor of his mother's house stood a quaintly carved black walnut bookcase, containing a small but remarkable collection of books, which had at one time been used, in his hours of retreat and relaxation from business and politics, by the distinguished gentleman who did not give his name to Mis' Molly's children,—to whom it would have been a valuable heritage, could they have had the right to bear it. Among the books were a volume of Fielding's complete works, in fine print, set in double columns; a set of Bulwer's novels; a collection of everything that Walter Scott—the literary idol of the South—had ever written; Beaumont and Fletcher's plays, cheek by jowl with the history of the virtuous Clarissa Harlowe; the Spectator and Tristram Shandy, Robinson Crusoe and the Arabian Nights. On these secluded shelves Roderick Random, Don Quixote, and Gil Blas for a long time ceased their wanderings, the Pilgrim's Progress was suspended, Milton's mighty harmonies were dumb, and Shakespeare reigned over a silent kingdom. An illustrated Bible, with a wonderful Apocrypha, was flanked on one side by Volney's Ruins of Empire and on the other by Paine's Age of Reason, for the collector of the books had been a man of catholic taste as well as of inquiring mind, and no one who could have criticised his reading ever penetrated behind the cedar hedge. A history of the French Revolution consorted amiably with a homespun chronicle of North Carolina, rich in biographical notices of distinguished citizens and inscriptions from their tombstones, upon reading which one might well wonder why North Carolina had not long ago eclipsed the rest of the world in wealth, wisdom, glory, and renown. On almost every page of this monumental work could be found the most ardent panegyrics of liberty, side by side with the slavery statistics of the State,—an incongruity of which, the learned author was deliciously unconscious.

When John Walden was yet a small boy, he had learned all that could be taught by the faded mulatto teacher in the long, shiny black frock coat, whom local public opinion permitted to teach a handful of free colored children for a pittance barely enough to keep soul and body together. When the boy had learned to read, he discovered the library, which for several years had been without a reader, and found in it the portal of a new world, peopled with strange and marvelous beings. Lying prone upon the floor of the shaded front piazza, behind the fragrant garden, he followed the fortunes of Tom Jones and Sophia; he wept over the fate of Eugene Aram; he penetrated with Richard the Lion-heart into Saladin's tent, with Gil Blas into the robbers' cave; he flew through the air on the magic carpet or the enchanted horse, or tied with Sindbad to the roc's leg. Sometimes he read or repeated the simpler stories to his little sister, sitting wide-eyed by his side. When he had read all the books,—indeed, long before he had read them all,—he too had tasted of the fruit of the Tree of Knowledge: contentment took its flight, and happiness lay far beyond the sphere where he was born. The blood of his white fathers, the heirs of the ages, cried out for its own, and after the manner of that blood set about getting the object of its desire.

Near the corner of Mackenzie Street, just one block north of the Patesville market-house, there had stood for many years before the war, on the verge of the steep bank of Beaver Creek, a small frame office building, the front of which was level with the street, while the rear rested on long brick pillars founded on the solid rock at the edge of the brawling stream below. Here, for nearly half a century, Archibald Straight had transacted legal business for the best people of Northumberland County. Full many a lawsuit had he won, lost, or settled; many a spendthrift had he saved from ruin, and not a few families from disgrace. Several times honored by election to the bench, he had so dispensed justice tempered with mercy as to win the hearts of all good citizens, and especially those of the poor, the oppressed, and the socially disinherited. The rights of the humblest negro, few as they might be, were as sacred to him as those of the proudest aristocrat, and he had sentenced a man to be hanged for the murder of his own slave. An old-fashioned man, tall and spare of figure and bowed somewhat with age, he was always correctly clad in a long frock coat of broadcloth, with a high collar and a black stock. Courtly in address to his social equals (superiors he had none), he was kind and considerate to those beneath him. He owned a few domestic servants, no one of whom had ever felt the weight of his hand, and for whose ultimate freedom he had provided in his will. In the long-drawn-out slavery agitation he had taken a keen interest, rather as observer than as participant. As the heat of controversy increased, his lack of zeal for the peculiar institution led to his defeat for the bench by a more active partisan. His was too just a mind not to perceive the arguments on both sides; but, on the whole, he had stood by the ancient landmarks, content to let events drift to a conclusion he did not expect to see; the institutions of his fathers would probably last his lifetime.

One day Judge Straight was sitting in his office reading a recently published pamphlet,—presenting an elaborate pro-slavery argument, based upon the hopeless intellectual inferiority of the negro, and the physical and moral degeneration of mulattoes, who combined the worst qualities of their two ancestral races,—when a barefooted boy walked into the office, straw hat in hand, came boldly up to the desk at which the old judge was sitting, and said as the judge looked up through his gold-rimmed glasses,—

"Sir, I want to be a lawyer!"

"God bless me!" exclaimed the judge. "It is a singular desire, from a singular source, and expressed in a singular way. Who the devil are you, sir, that wish so strange a thing as to become a lawyer—everybody's servant?"

"And everybody's master, sir," replied the lad stoutly.

"That is a matter of opinion, and open to argument," rejoined the judge, amused and secretly flattered by this tribute to his profession, "though there may be a grain of truth in what you say, But what is your name, Mr. Would-be-lawyer?"

"John Walden, sir," answered the lad.

"John Walden?—Walden?" mused the judge. "What Walden can that be? Do you belong in town?"

"Yes, sir."

"Humph! I can't imagine who you are. It's plain that you are a lad of good blood, and yet I don't know whose son you can be. What is your father's name?"

The lad hesitated, and flushed crimson.

The old gentleman noted his hesitation. "It is a wise son," he thought, "that knows his own father. He is a bright lad, and will have this question put to him more than once. I 'll see how he will answer it."

The boy maintained an awkward silence, while the old judge eyed him keenly.

"My father's dead," he said at length, in a low voice. "I 'm Mis' Molly Walden's son." He had expected, of course, to tell who he was, if asked, but had not foreseen just the form of the inquiry; and while he had thought more of his race than of his illegitimate birth, he realized at this moment as never before that this question too would be always with him. As put now by Judge Straight, it made him wince. He had not read his father's books for nothing.

"God bless my soul!" exclaimed the judge in genuine surprise at this answer; "and you want to be a lawyer!" The situation was so much worse than he had suspected that even an old practitioner, case-hardened by years of life at the trial table and on the bench, was startled for a moment into a comical sort of consternation, so apparent that a lad less stout-hearted would have weakened and fled at the sight of it.

"Yes, sir. Why not?" responded the boy, trembling a little at the knees, but stoutly holding his ground.

"He wants to be a lawyer, and he asks me why not!" muttered the judge, speaking apparently to himself. He rose from his chair, walked across the room, and threw open a window. The cool morning air brought with it the babbling of the stream below and the murmur of the mill near by. He glanced across the creek to the ruined foundation of an old house on the low ground beyond the creek. Turning from the window, he looked back at the boy, who had remained standing between him and the door. At that moment another lad came along the street and stopped opposite the open doorway. The presence of the two boys in connection with the book he had been reading suggested a comparison. The judge knew the lad outside as the son of a leading merchant of the town. The merchant and his wife were both of old families which had lived in the community for several generations, and whose blood was presumably of the purest strain; yet the boy was sallow, with amorphous features, thin shanks, and stooping shoulders. The youth, standing in the judge's office, on the contrary, was straight, shapely, and well-grown. His eye was clear, and he kept it fixed on the old gentleman with a look in which there was nothing of cringing. He was no darker than many a white boy bronzed by the Southern sun; his hair and eyes were black, and his features of the high-bred, clean-cut order that marks the patrician type the world over. What struck the judge most forcibly, however, was the lad's resemblance to an old friend and companion and client. He recalled a certain conversation with this old friend, who had said to him one day:

"Archie, I'm coming in to have you draw my will. There are some children for whom I would like to make ample provision. I can't give them anything else, but money will make them free of the world."

The judge's friend had died suddenly before carrying out this good intention. The judge had taken occasion to suggest the existence of these children, and their father's intentions concerning them, to the distant relatives who had inherited his friend's large estate. They had chosen to take offense at the suggestion. One had thought it in shocking bad taste; another considered any mention of such a subject an insult to his cousin's memory. A third had said, with flashing eyes, that the woman and her children had already robbed the estate of enough; that it was a pity the little niggers were not slaves—that they would have added measurably to the value of the property. Judge Straight's manner indicated some disapproval of their attitude, and the settlement of the estate was placed in other hands than his. Now, this son, with his father's face and his father's voice, stood before his father's friend, demanding entrance to the golden gate of opportunity, which society barred to all who bore the blood of the despised race.

As he kept on looking at the boy, who began at length to grow somewhat embarrassed under this keen scrutiny, the judge's mind reverted to certain laws and judicial decisions that he had looked up once or twice in his lifetime. Even the law, the instrument by which tyranny riveted the chains upon its victims, had revolted now and then against the senseless and unnatural prejudice by which a race ascribing its superiority to right of blood permitted a mere suspicion of servile blood to outweigh a vast preponderance of its own.

"Why, indeed, should he not be a lawyer, or anything else that a man might be, if it be in him?" asked the judge, speaking rather to himself than to the boy. "Sit down," he ordered, pointing to a chair on the other side of the room. That he should ask a colored lad to be seated in his presence was of itself enough to stamp the judge as eccentric. "You want to be a lawyer," he went on, adjusting his spectacles. "You are aware, of course, that you are a negro?"

"I am white," replied the lad, turning back his sleeve and holding out his arm, "and I am free, as all my people were before me."

The old lawyer shook his head, and fixed his eyes upon the lad with a slightly quizzical smile, "You are black," he said, "and you are not free. You cannot travel without your papers; you cannot secure accommodations at an inn; you could not vote, if you were of age; you cannot be out after nine o'clock without a permit. If a white man struck you, you could not return the blow, and you could not testify against him in a court of justice. You are black, my lad, and you are not free. Did you ever hear of the Dred Scott decision, delivered by the great, wise, and learned Judge Taney?"

"No, sir," answered the boy.

"It is too long to read," rejoined the judge, taking up the pamphlet he had laid down upon the lad's entrance, "but it says in substance, as quoted by this author, that negroes are beings 'of an inferior order, and altogether unfit to associate with the white race, either in social or political relations; in fact, so inferior that they have no rights which the white man is bound to respect, and that the negro may justly and lawfully be reduced to slavery for his benefit.' That is the law of this nation, and that is the reason why you cannot be a lawyer."

"It may all be true," replied the boy, "but it don't apply to me. It says 'the negro.' A negro is black; I am white, and not black."

"Black as ink, my lad," returned the lawyer, shaking his head. "'One touch of nature makes the whole world kin,' says the poet. Somewhere, sometime, you had a black ancestor. One drop of black blood makes the whole man black."

"Why should n't it be the other way, if the white blood is so much superior?" inquired the lad.

"Because it is more convenient as it is—and more profitable."

"It is not right," maintained the lad.

"God bless me!" exclaimed the old gentleman, "he is invading the field of ethics! He will be questioning the righteousness of slavery next! I'm afraid you would n't make a good lawyer, in any event. Lawyers go by the laws—they abide by the accomplished fact; to them, whatever is, is right. The laws do not permit men of color to practice law, and public sentiment would not allow one of them to study it."

"I had thought," said the lad, "that I might pass for white. There are white people darker than I am."

"Ah, well, that is another matter; but"—

The judge stopped for a moment, struck by the absurdity of his arguing such a question with a mulatto boy. He really must be falling into premature dotage. The proper thing would be to rebuke the lad for his presumption and advise him to learn to take care of horses, or make boots, or lay bricks. But again he saw his old friend in the lad's face, and again he looked in vain for any sign of negro blood. The least earmark would have turned the scale, but he could not find it.

"That is another matter," he repeated. "Here you have started as black, and must remain so. But if you wish to move away, and sink your past into oblivion, the case might be different. Let us see what the law is; you might not need it if you went far enough, but it is well enough to be within it—liberty is sweeter when founded securely on the law."

He took down a volume bound in legal calf and glanced through it. "The color line is drawn in North Carolina at four generations removed from the negro; there have been judicial decisions to that effect. I imagine that would cover your case. But let us see what South Carolina may say about it," he continued, taking another book. "I think the law is even more liberal there. Ah, this is the place:—

"'The term mulatto,'" he read, "is not invariably applicable to every admixture of African blood with the European, nor is one having all the features of a white to be ranked with the degraded class designated by the laws of this State as persons of color, because of some remote taint of the negro race. Juries would probably be justified in holding a person to be white in whom the admixture of African blood did not exceed one eighth. And even where color or feature are doubtful, it is a question for the jury to decide by reputation, by reception into society, and by their exercise of the privileges of the white man, as well as by admixture of blood.'"

"Then I need not be black?" the boy cried, with sparkling eyes.

"No," replied the lawyer, "you need not be black, away from Patesville. You have the somewhat unusual privilege, it seems, of choosing between two races, and if you are a lad of spirit, as I think you are, it will not take you long to make your choice. As you have all the features of a white man, you would, at least in South Carolina, have simply to assume the place and exercise the privileges of a white man. You might, of course, do the same thing anywhere, as long as no one knew your origin. But the matter has been adjudicated there in several cases, and on the whole I think South Carolina is the place for you. They're more liberal there, perhaps because they have many more blacks than whites, and would like to lessen the disproportion."

"From this time on," said the boy, "I am white."

"Softly, softly, my Caucasian fellow citizen," returned the judge, chuckling with quiet amusement. "You are white in the abstract, before the law. You may cherish the fact in secret, but I would not advise you to proclaim it openly just yet. You must wait until you go away—to South Carolina."

"And can I learn to be a lawyer, sir?" asked the lad.

"It seems to me that you ought to be reasonably content for one day with what you have learned already. You cannot be a lawyer until you are white, in position as well as in theory, nor until you are twenty-one years old. I need an office boy. If you are willing to come into my office, sweep it, keep my books dusted, and stay here when I am out, I do not care. To the rest of the town you will be my servant, and still a negro. If you choose to read my books when no one is about and be white in your own private opinion, I have no objection. When you have made up your mind to go away, perhaps what you have read may help you. But mum's the word! If I hear a whisper of this from any other source, out you go, neck and crop! I am willing to help you make a man of yourself, but it can only be done under the rose."

For two years John Walden openly swept the office and surreptitiously read the law books of old Judge

Straight. When he was eighteen, he asked his mother for a sum of money, kissed her good-by, and went out into the world. When his sister, then a pretty child of seven, cried because her big brother was going away, he took her up in his arms, gave her a silver dime with a hole in it for a keepsake, hugged her close, and kissed her.

"Nev' min', sis," he said soothingly. "Be a good little gal, an' some o' these days I'll come back to see you and bring you somethin' fine."

In after years, when Mis' Molly was asked what had become of her son, she would reply with sad complacency,—

"He's gone over on the other side."

As we have seen, he came back ten years later.

Many years before, when Mis' Molly, then a very young woman, had taken up her residence in the house behind the cedars, the gentleman heretofore referred to had built a cabin on the opposite corner, in which he had installed a trusted slave by the name of Peter Fowler and his wife Nancy. Peter was a good mechanic, and hired his time from his master with the provision that Peter and his wife should do certain work for Mis' Molly and serve as a sort of protection for her. In course of time Peter, who was industrious and thrifty, saved enough money to purchase his freedom and that of his wife and their one child, and to buy the little house across the street, with the cooper shop behind it. After they had acquired their freedom, Peter and Nancy did no work for Mis' Molly save as they were paid for it, and as a rule preferred not to work at all for the woman who had been practically their mistress; it made them seem less free.

Nevertheless, the two households had remained upon good terms, even after the death of the man whose will had brought them together, and who had remained Peter's patron after he had ceased to be his master. There was no intimate association between the two families. Mis' Molly felt herself infinitely superior to Peter and his wife,—scarcely less superior than her poor white neighbors felt themselves to Mis' Molly. Mis' Molly always meant to be kind, and treated Peter and Nancy with a certain good-natured condescension. They resented this, never openly or offensively, but always in a subconscious sort of way, even when they did not speak of it among themselves—much as they had resented her mistress-ship in the old days. For after all, they argued, in spite of her airs and graces, her white face and her fine clothes, was she not a negro, even as themselves? and since the slaves had been freed, was not one negro as good as another?

Peter's son Frank had grown up with little Rena. He was several years older than she, and when Rena was a small child Mis' Molly had often confided her to his care, and he had watched over her and kept her from harm. When Frank became old enough to go to work in the cooper shop, Rena, then six or seven, had often gone across to play among the clean white shavings. Once Frank, while learning the trade, had let slip a sharp steel tool, which flying toward Rena had grazed her arm and sent the red blood coursing along the white flesh and soaking the muslin sleeve. He had rolled up the sleeve and stanched the blood and dried her tears. For a long time thereafter her mother kept her away from the shop and was very cold to Frank. One day the little girl wandered down to the bank of the old canal. It had been raining for several days, and the water was quite deep in the channel. The child slipped and fell into the stream. From the open window of the cooper shop Frank heard a scream. He ran down to the canal and pulled her out, and carried her all wet and dripping to the house. From that time he had been restored to favor. He had watched the girl grow up to womanhood in the years following the war, and had been sorry when she became too old to play about the shop.

He never spoke to her of love,—indeed, he never thought of his passion in such a light. There would have been no legal barrier to their union; there would have been no frightful menace to white supremacy in the marriage of the negro and the octoroon: the drop of dark blood bridged the chasm. But Frank knew that she did not love him, and had not hoped that she might. His was one of those rare souls that can give with small hope of return. When he had made the scar upon her arm, by the same token she had branded him her slave forever; when he had saved her from a watery grave, he had given his life to her. There are depths of fidelity and devotion in the negro heart that have never been fathomed or fully appreciated. Now and then in the kindlier phases of slavery these qualities were brightly conspicuous, and in them, if wisely appealed to, lies the strongest hope of amity between the two races whose destiny seems bound up together in the Western world. Even a dumb brute can be won by kindness. Surely it were worth while to try some other weapon than scorn and contumely and hard words upon people of our common race,—the human race, which is bigger and broader than Celt or

Saxon, barbarian or Greek, Jew or Gentile, black or white; for we are all children of a common Father, forget it as we may, and each one of us is in some measure his brother's keeper.

XIX
GOD MADE US ALL

RENA was convalescent from a two-weeks' illness when her brother came to see her. He arrived at Patesville by an early morning train before the town was awake, and walked unnoticed from the station to his mother's house. His meeting with his sister was not without emotion: he embraced her tenderly, and Rena became for a few minutes a very Niobe of grief.

"Oh, it was cruel, cruel!" she sobbed. "I shall never get over it."

"I know it, my dear," replied Warwick soothingly,—"I know it, and I'm to blame for it. If I had never taken you away from here, you would have escaped this painful experience. But do not despair; all is not lost. Tryon will not marry you, as I hoped he might, while I feared the contrary; but he is a gentleman, and will be silent. Come back and try again."

"No, John. I could n't go through it a second time. I managed very well before, when I thought our secret was unknown; but now I could never be sure. It would be borne on every wind, for aught I knew, and every rustling leaf might whisper it. The law, you said, made us white; but not the law, nor even love, can conquer prejudice. *He* spoke of my beauty, my grace, My sweetness! I looked into his eyes and believed him. And yet he left me without a word! What would I do in Clarence now? I came away engaged to be married, with even the day set; I should go back forsaken and discredited; even the servants would pity me."

"Little Albert is pining for you," suggested Warwick. "We could make some explanation that would spare your feelings."

"Ah, do not tempt me, John! I love the child, and am grieved to leave him. I'm grateful, too, John, for what you have done for me. I am not sorry that I tried it. It opened my eyes, and I would rather die of knowledge than live in ignorance. But I could not go through it again, John; I am not strong enough. I could do you no good; I have made you trouble enough already. Get a mother for Albert—Mrs. Newberry would marry you, secret and all, and would be good to the child. Forget me, John, and take care of yourself. Your friend has found you out through me—he may have told a dozen people. You think he will be silent;—I thought he loved me, and he left me without a word, and with a look that told me how he hated and despised me. I would not have believed it— even of a white man."

"You do him an injustice," said her brother, producing Tryon's letter. "He did not get off unscathed. He sent you a message."

She turned her face away, but listened while be read the letter. "He did not love me," she cried angrily, when he had finished, "or he would not have cast me off—he would not have looked at me so. The law would have let him marry me. I seemed as white as he did. He might have gone anywhere with me, and no one would have stared at us curiously; no one need have known. The world is wide—there must be some place where a man could live happily with the woman he loved."

"Yes, Rena, there is; and the world is wide enough for you to get along without Tryon."

"For a day or two," she went on, "I hoped he might come back. But his expression in that awful moment grew upon me, haunted me day and night, until I shuddered at the thought that I might ever see him again. He looked at me as though I were not even a human being. I do not love him any longer, John; I would not marry him if I were white, or he were as I am. He did not love me—or he would have acted differently. He might have loved me and have left me—he could not have loved me and have looked at me so!"

She was weeping hysterically. There was little he could say to comfort her. Presently she dried her tears. Warwick was reluctant to leave her in Patesville. Her childish happiness had been that of ignorance; she could never be happy there again. She had flowered in the sunlight; she must not pine away in the shade.

"If you won't come back with me, Rena, I 'll send you to some school at the North, where you can acquire a liberal education, and prepare yourself for some career of usefulness. You may marry a better man than even Tryon."

"No," she replied firmly, "I shall never marry any man, and I 'll not leave mother again. God is against it; I'll stay with my own people."

"God has nothing to do with it," retorted Warwick.

"God is too often a convenient stalking-horse for human selfishness. If there is anything to be done, so unjust, so despicable, so wicked that human reason revolts at it, there is always some smug hypocrite to exclaim, 'It is the will of God.'"

"God made us all," continued Rena dreamily, "and for some good purpose, though we may not always see it. He made some people white, and strong, and masterful, and—heartless. He made others black and homely, and poor and weak"—

"And a lot of others 'poor white' and shiftless," smiled Warwick.

"He made us, too," continued Rena, intent upon her own thought, "and He must have had a reason for it. Perhaps He meant us to bring the others together in his own good time. A man may make a new place for himself—a woman is born and bound to hers. God must have meant me to stay here, or He would not have sent me back. I shall accept things as they are. Why should I seek the society of people whose friendship—and love—one little word can turn to scorn? I was right, John; I ought to have told him. Suppose he had married me and then had found it out?"

To Rena's argument of divine foreordination Warwick attached no weight whatever. He had seen God's heel planted for four long years upon the land which had nourished slavery. Had God ordained the crime that the punishment might follow? It would have been easier for Omnipotence to prevent the crime. The experience of his sister had stirred up a certain bitterness against white people—a feeling which he had put aside years ago, with his dark blood, but which sprang anew into life when the fact of his own origin was brought home to him so forcibly through his sister's misfortune. His sworn friend and promised brother-in-law had thrown him over promptly, upon the discovery of the hidden drop of dark blood. How many others of his friends would do the same, if they but knew of it? He had begun to feel a little of the spiritual estrangement from his associates that he had noticed in Rena during her life at Clarence. The fact that several persons knew his secret had spoiled the fine flavor of perfect security hitherto marking his position. George Tryon was a man of honor among white men, and had deigned to extend the protection of his honor to Warwick as a man, though no longer as a friend; to Rena as a woman, but not as a wife. Tryon, however, was only human, and who could tell when their paths in life might cross again, or what future temptation Tryon might feel to use a damaging secret to their disadvantage? Warwick had cherished certain ambitions, but these he must now put behind him. In the obscurity of private life, his past would be of little moment; in the glare of a political career, one's antecedents are public property, and too great a reserve in regard to one's past is regarded as a confession of something discreditable. Frank, too, knew the secret—a good, faithful fellow, even where there was no obligation of fidelity; he ought to do something for Frank to show their appreciation of his conduct. But what assurance was there that Frank would always be discreet about the affairs of others? Judge Straight knew the whole story, and old men are sometimes garrulous. Dr. Green suspected the secret; he had a wife and daughters. If old Judge Straight could have known Warwick's thoughts, he would have realized the fulfillment of his prophecy. Warwick, who had builded so well for himself, had weakened the structure of his own life by trying to share his good fortune with his sister.

"Listen, Rena," he said, with a sudden impulse, "we'll go to the North or West—I 'll go with you—far away from the South and the Southern people, and start life over again. It will be easier for you, it will not be hard for me—I am young, and have means. There are no strong ties to bind me to the South. I would have a larger outlook elsewhere."

"And what about our mother?" asked Rena.

It would be necessary to leave her behind, they both perceived clearly enough, unless they were prepared to surrender the advantage of their whiteness and drop back to the lower rank. The mother bore the mark of the Ethiopian—not pronouncedly, but distinctly; neither would Mis' Molly, in all probability, care to leave home and friends and the graves of her loved ones. She had no mental resources to supply the place of these; she was, moreover, too old to be transplanted; she would not fit into Warwick's scheme for a new life.

"I left her once," said Rena, "and it brought pain and sorrow to all three of us. She is not strong, and I will not leave her here to die alone. This shall be my home while she lives, and if I leave it again, it shall be for only a short time, to go where I can write to her freely, and hear from her often. Don't worry about me, John,—I shall do very well."

Warwick sighed. He was sincerely sorry to leave his sister, and yet he saw that for the time being her resolution was not to be shaken. He must bide his time. Perhaps, in a few months, she would tire of the old life. His door would be always open to her, and he would charge himself with her future.

"Well, then," he said, concluding the argument, "we'll say no more about it for the present. I 'll write to you later. I was afraid that you might not care to go back just now, and so I brought your trunk along with me."

He gave his mother the baggage-check. She took it across to Frank, who, during the day, brought the trunk from the depot. Mis' Molly offered to pay him for the service, but he would accept nothing.

"Lawd, no, Mis' Molly; I did n' hafter go out'n my way ter git dat trunk. I had a load er sperritbairls ter haul ter de still, an' de depot wuz right on my way back. It 'd be robbin' you ter take pay fer a little thing lack dat."

"My son John 's here," said Mis' Molly "an' he wants to see you. Come into the settin'-room. We don't want folks to know he 's in town; but you know all our secrets, an' we can trust you like one er the family."

"I'm glad to see you again, Frank," said Warwick, extending his hand and clasping Frank's warmly. "You've grown up since I saw you last, but it seems you are still our good friend."

"Our very good friend," interjected Rena.

Frank threw her a grateful glance. "Yas, suh," he said, looking Warwick over with a friendly eye, "an' you is growed some, too. I seed you, you know, down dere where you live; but I did n' let on, fer you an' Mis' Rena wuz w'ite as anybody; an' eve'ybody said you wuz good ter cullud folks, an' he'ped 'em in deir lawsuits an' one way er 'nuther, an' I wuz jes' plum' glad ter see you gettin' 'long so fine, dat I wuz, certain sho', an' no mistake about it."

"Thank you, Frank, and I want you to understand how much I appreciate"—

"How much we all appreciate," corrected Rena.

"Yes, how much we all appreciate, and how grateful we all are for your kindness to mother for so many years. I know from her and from my sister how good you've been to them."

"Lawd, suh!" returned Frank deprecatingly, "you 're makin' a mountain out'n a molehill. I ain't done nuthin' ter speak of—not half ez much ez I would 'a' done. I wuz glad ter do w'at little I could, fer frien'ship's sake."

"We value your friendship, Frank, and we'll not forget it."

"No, Frank," added Rena, "we will never forget it, and you shall always be our good friend."

Frank left the room and crossed the street with swelling heart. He would have given his life for Rena. A kind word was doubly sweet from her lips; no service would be too great to pay for her friendship.

When Frank went out to the stable next morning to feed his mule, his eyes opened wide with astonishment. In place of the decrepit, one-eyed army mule he had put up the night before, a fat, sleek specimen of vigorous mulehood greeted his arrival with the sonorous hehaw of lusty youth. Hanging on a peg near by was a set of fine new harness, and standing under the adjoining shed, as he perceived, a handsome new cart.

"Well, well!" exclaimed Frank; "ef I did n' mos' know whar dis mule, an' dis kyart, an' dis harness come from, I'd 'low dere'd be'n witcheraf' er cunjin' wukkin' here. But, oh my, dat is a fine mule!—I mos' wush I could keep 'im."

He crossed the road to the house behind the cedars, and found Mis' Molly in the kitchen.

"Mis' Molly," he protested, "I ain't done nuthin' ter deserve dat mule. W'at little I done fer you wa'n't done fer pay. I 'd ruther not keep dem things."

"Fer goodness' sake, Frank!" exclaimed his neighbor, with a well-simulated air of mystification, "what are you talkin' about?"

"You knows w'at I 'm talkin' about, Mis' Molly; you knows well ernuff I'm talkin' about dat fine mule an' kyart an' harness over dere in my stable."

"How should I know anything about 'em?" she asked.

"Now, Mis' Molly! You folks is jes' tryin' ter fool me, an' make me take somethin' fer nuthin'. I lef' my ole mule an' kyart an' harness in de stable las' night, an' dis mawnin' dey're gone, an' new ones in deir place. Co'se you knows whar dey come from!"

"Well, now, Frank, sence you mention it, I did see a witch flyin' roun' here las' night on a broomstick, an' it 'peared ter me she lit on yo'r barn, an' I s'pose she turned yo'r old things into new ones. I would n't bother my mind about it if I was you, for she may turn 'em back any night, you know; an' you might as well have the use of 'em in the mean while."

"Dat's all foolishness, Mis' Molly, an' I'm gwine ter fetch dat mule right over here an' tell yo' son ter gimme my ole one back."

"My son 's gone," she replied, "an' I don't know nothin' about yo'r old mule. And what would I do with a mule, anyhow? I ain't got no barn to put him in."

"I suspect you don't care much for us after all, Frank," said Rena reproachfully—she had come in while they were talking. "You meet with a piece of good luck, and you 're afraid of it, lest it might have come from us."

"Now, Miss Rena, you ought n't ter say dat," expostulated Frank, his reluctance yielding immediately. "I'll keep de mule an' de kyart an' de harness—fac', I'll have ter keep 'em, 'cause I ain't got no others. But dey 're gwine ter be yo'n ez much ez mine. W'enever you wants anything hauled, er wants yo' lot ploughed, er anything— dat's yo' mule, an' I'm yo' man an' yo' mammy's."

So Frank went back to the stable, where he feasted his eyes on his new possessions, fed and watered the mule, and curried and brushed his coat until it shone like a looking-glass.

"Now dat," remarked Peter, at the breakfast-table, when informed of the transaction, "is somethin' lack rale w'ite folks."

No real white person had ever given Peter a mule or a cart. He had rendered one of them unpaid service for half a lifetime, and had paid for the other half; and some of them owed him substantial sums for work performed. But "to him that hath shall be given"—Warwick paid for the mule, and the real white folks got most of the credit.

XX
DIGGING UP ROOTS

WHEN the first great shock of his discovery wore off, the fact of Rena's origin lost to Tryon some of its initial repugnance—indeed, the repugnance was not to the woman at all, as their past relations were evidence, but merely to the thought of her as a wife. It could hardly have failed to occur to so reasonable a man as Tryon that Rena's case could scarcely be unique. Surely in the past centuries of free manners and easy morals that had prevailed in remote parts of the South, there must have been many white persons whose origin would not have borne too microscopic an investigation. Family trees not seldom have a crooked branch; or, to use a more apposite figure, many a flock has its black sheep. Being a man of lively imagination, Tryon soon found himself putting all sorts of hypothetical questions about a matter which he had already definitely determined. If he had married Rena in ignorance of her secret, and had learned it afterwards, would he have put her aside? If, knowing her history, he had nevertheless married her, and she had subsequently displayed some trait of character that would suggest the negro, could he have forgotten or forgiven the taint? Could he still have held her in love and honor? If not, could he have given her the outward seeming of affection, or could he have been more than coldly tolerant? He was glad that he had been spared this ordeal. With an effort he put the whole matter definitely and conclusively aside, as he had done a hundred times already.

Returning to his home, after an absence of several months in South Carolina, it was quite apparent to his mother's watchful eye that he was in serious trouble. He was absent-minded, monosyllabic, sighed deeply and often, and could not always conceal the traces of secret tears. For Tryon was young, and possessed of a sensitive soul—a source of happiness or misery, as the Fates decree. To those thus dowered, the heights of rapture are accessible, the abysses of despair yawn threateningly; only the dull monotony of contentment is denied.

Mrs. Tryon vainly sought by every gentle art a woman knows to win her son's confidence. "What is the matter, George, dear?" she would ask, stroking his hot brow with her small, cool hand as he sat moodily nursing his grief. "Tell your mother, George. Who else could comfort you so well as she?"

"Oh, it 's nothing, mother,—nothing at all," he would reply, with a forced attempt at lightness. "It's only your fond imagination, you best of mothers."

It was Mrs. Tryon's turn to sigh and shed a clandestine tear. Until her son had gone away on this trip to South Carolina, he had kept no secrets from her: his heart had been an open book, of which she knew every page; now, some painful story was inscribed therein which he meant she should not read. If she could have abdicated her empire to Blanche Leary or have shared it with her, she would have yielded gracefully; but very palpably some other influence than Blanche's had driven joy from her son's countenance and lightness from his heart.

Miss Blanche Leary, whom Tryon found in the house upon his return, was a demure, pretty little blonde, with an amiable disposition, a talent for society, and a pronounced fondness for George Tryon. A poor girl, of an excellent family impoverished by the war, she was distantly related to Mrs. Tryon, had for a long time enjoyed that lady's favor, and was her choice for George's wife when he should be old enough to marry. A woman less interested than Miss Leary would have perceived that there was something wrong with Tryon. Miss Leary had no doubt that there was a woman at the bottom of it,— for about what else should youth worry but love? or if one's love affairs run smoothly, why should one worry about anything at all? Miss Leary, in the nineteen years of her mundane existence, had not been without mild experiences of the heart, and had hovered for some time on the verge of disappointment with respect to Tryon himself. A sensitive pride would have driven more than one woman away at the sight of the man of her preference sighing like a furnace for some absent fair one. But Mrs. Tryon was so cordial, and insisted so strenuously upon her remaining, that Blanche's love, which was strong, conquered her pride, which was no more than a reasonable young woman ought to have who sets success above mere sentiment. She remained in the house and bided her opportunity. If George practically ignored her for a time, she did not throw herself at all in his way. She went on a visit to some girls in the neighborhood and remained away a week, hoping that she might be missed. Tryon expressed no regret at her departure and no particular satisfaction upon her return. If the house was duller in her absence, he was but dimly conscious of the difference. He was still fighting a battle in which a susceptible heart and a reasonable mind had locked horns in a well-nigh hopeless conflict. Reason, common-sense, the instinctive ready-made judgments of his training and environment,—the deep-seated prejudices of race and caste,—commanded him to dismiss Rena from his thoughts. His stubborn heart simply would not let go.

XXI
A GILDED OPPORTUNITY

ALTHOUGH the whole fabric of Rena's new life toppled and fell with her lover's defection, her sympathies, broadened by culture and still more by her recent emotional experience, did not shrink, as would have been the case with a more selfish soul, to the mere limits of her personal sorrow, great as this seemed at the moment. She had learned to love, and when the love of one man failed her, she turned to humanity, as a stream obstructed in its course overflows the adjacent country. Her early training had not directed her thoughts to the darker people with whose fate her own was bound up so closely, but rather away from them. She had been taught to despise them because they were not so white as she was, and had been slaves while she was free. Her life in her brother's home, by removing her from immediate contact with them, had given her a different point of view,—one which emphasized their shortcomings, and thereby made vastly clearer to her the gulf that separated them from the new world in which she lived; so that when misfortune threw her back upon them, the reaction brought her nearer than before. Where once she had seemed able to escape from them, they were now, it appeared, her inalienable race. Thus doubly equipped, she was able to view them at once with the mental eye of an outsider and the sympathy of a sister: she could see their faults, and judge them charitably; she knew and appreciated their good qualities. With her quickened intelligence she could perceive how great was their need and how small their opportunity; and with this illumination came the desire to contribute to their help. She had not the breadth or culture to see in all its ramifications the great problem which still puzzles statesmen and philosophers; but she was conscious of the wish, and of the power, in a small way, to do something for the advancement of those who had just set their feet upon the ladder of progress.

This new-born desire to be of service to her rediscovered people was not long without an opportunity for expression. Yet the Fates willed that her future should be but another link in a connected chain: she was to be as powerless to put aside her recent past as she had been to escape from the influence of her earlier life. There are sordid souls that eat and drink and breed and die, and imagine they have lived. But Rena's life since her great awakening had been that of the emotions, and her temperament made of it a continuous life. Her successive states of consciousness were not detachable, but united to form a single if not an entirely harmonious whole. To her sensitive spirit to-day was born of yesterday, to-morrow would be but the offspring of to-day.

One day, along toward noon, her mother received a visit from Mary B. Pettifoot, a second cousin, who lived on Back Street, only a short distance from the house behind the cedars. Rena had gone out, so that the visitor found Mis' Molly alone.

"I heared you say, Cousin Molly," said Mary B. (no one ever knew what the B. in Mary's name stood for,—it was a mere ornamental flourish), "that Rena was talkin' 'bout teachin' school. I've got a good chance fer her, ef she keers ter take it. My cousin Jeff Wain 'rived in town this mo'nin', f'm 'way down in Sampson County, ter git a teacher fer the nigger school in his deestric'. I s'pose he

160

mought 'a' got one f'm 'roun' Newbern, er Goldsboro, er some er them places eas', but he 'lowed he'd like to visit some er his kin an' ole frien's, an' so kill two birds with one stone."

"I seed a strange mulatter man, with a bay hoss an' a new buggy, drivin' by here this mo'nin' early, from down to'ds the river," rejoined Mis' Molly. "I wonder if that wuz him?"

"Did he have on a linen duster?" asked Mary B.

"Yas, an' 'peared to be a very well sot up man," replied Mis' Molly, "'bout thirty-five years old, I should reckon."

"That wuz him," assented Mary B. "He's got a fine hoss an' buggy, an' a gol' watch an' chain, an' a big plantation, an' lots er hosses an' mules an' cows an' hawgs. He raise' fifty bales er cotton las' year, an' he's be'n ter the legislatur'."

"My gracious!" exclaimed Mis' Molly, struck with awe at this catalogue of the stranger's possessions—he was evidently worth more than a great many "rich" white people,—all white people in North Carolina in those days were either "rich" or "poor," the distinction being one of caste rather than of wealth. "Is he married?" she inquired with interest?

"No,—single. You mought 'low it was quare that he should n' be married at his age; but he was crossed in love oncet,"—Mary B. heaved a self-conscious sigh,—"an' has stayed single ever sence. That wuz ten years ago, but as some husban's is long-lived, an' there ain' no mo' chance fer 'im now than there wuz then, I reckon some nice gal mought stan' a good show er ketchin' 'im, ef she'd play her kyards right."

To Mis' Molly this was news of considerable importance. She had not thought a great deal of Rena's plan to teach; she considered it lowering for Rena, after having been white, to go among the negroes any more than was unavoidable. This opportunity, however, meant more than mere employment for her daughter. She had felt Rena's disappointment keenly, from the practical point of view, and, blaming herself for it, held herself all the more bound to retrieve the misfortune in any possible way. If she had not been sick, Rena would not have dreamed the fateful dream that had brought her to Patesville; for the connection between the vision and the reality was even closer in Mis' Molly's eyes than in Rena's. If the mother had not sent the letter announcing her illness and confirming the dream, Rena would not have ruined her promising future by coming to Patesville. But the harm had been done, and she was responsible, ignorantly of course, but none the less truly, and it only remained for her to make amends, as far as possible. Her highest ambition, since Rena had grown up, had been to see her married and comfortably settled in life. She had no hope that Tryon would come back. Rena had declared that she would make no further effort to get away from her people; and, furthermore, that she would never marry. To this latter statement Mis' Molly secretly attached but little importance. That a woman should go single from the cradle to the grave did not accord with her experience in life of the customs of North Carolina. She respected a grief she could not entirely fathom, yet did not for a moment believe that Rena would remain unmarried.

"You'd better fetch him roun' to see me, Ma'y B.," she said, "an' let 's see what he looks like. I'm pertic'lar 'bout my gal. She says she ain't goin' to marry nobody; but of co'se we know that's all foolishness."

"I'll fetch him roun' this evenin' 'bout three o'clock," said the visitor, rising. "I mus' hurry back now an' keep him comp'ny. Tell Rena ter put on her bes' bib an' tucker; for Mr. Wain is pertic'lar too, an' I've already be'n braggin' 'bout her looks."

When Mary B., at the appointed hour, knocked at Mis' Molly's front door,—the visit being one of ceremony, she had taken her cousin round to the Front Street entrance and through the flower garden,—Mis' Molly was prepared to receive them. After a decent interval, long enough to suggest that she had not been watching their approach and was not over-eager about the visit, she answered the knock and admitted them into the parlor. Mr. Wain was formally introduced, and seated himself on the ancient haircloth sofa, under the framed fashion-plate, while Mary B. sat by the open door and fanned herself with a palm-leaf fan.

Mis' Molly's impression of Wain was favorable. His complexion was of a light brown—not quite so fair as Mis' Molly would have preferred; but any deficiency in this regard, or in the matter of the stranger's features, which, while not unpleasing, leaned toward the broad mulatto type, was more than compensated in her eyes by very straight black hair, and, as soon appeared, a great facility of complimentary speech. On his introduction Mr. Wain bowed low, assumed an air of great admiration, and expressed his extreme delight in making the acquaintance of so distinguished-looking a lady.

"You're flatt'rin' me, Mr. Wain," returned Mis' Molly, with a gratified smile. "But you want to meet my daughter befo' you commence th'owin' bokays. Excuse my leavin' you—I 'll go an' fetch her."

She returned in a moment, followed by Rena. "Mr. Wain, 'low me to int'oduce you to my daughter Rena. Rena, this is Ma'y B.'s cousin on her pappy's side, who's come up from Sampson to git a school-teacher."

Rena bowed gracefully. Wain stared a moment in genuine astonishment, and then bent himself nearly double, keeping his eyes fixed meanwhile upon Rena's face. He had expected to see a pretty yellow girl, but had been prepared for no such radiant vision of beauty as this which now confronted him.

"Does—does you mean ter say, Mis' Walden, dat—dat dis young lady is yo' own daughter?" he stammered, rallying his forces for action.

"Why not, Mr. Wain?" asked Mis' Molly, bridling with mock resentment. "Do you mean ter 'low that she wuz changed in her cradle, er is she too good-lookin' to be my daughter?"

"My deah Mis' Walden! it 'ud be wastin' wo'ds fer me ter say dat dey ain' no young lady too good-lookin' ter be yo' daughter; but you 're lookin' so young yo'sef dat I'd ruther take her fer yo' sister."

"Yas," rejoined Mis' Molly, with animation, "they ain't many years between us. I wuz ruther young myself when she wuz bo'n."

"An', mo'over," Wain went on, "it takes me a minute er so ter git my min' use' ter thinkin' er Mis' Rena as a cullud young lady. I mought 'a' seed her a hund'ed times, an' I'd 'a' never dreamt but w'at she wuz a w'ite young lady, f'm one er do bes' families."

"Yas, Mr. Wain," replied Mis' Molly complacently, "all

three er my child'en wuz white, an' one of 'em has be'n on the other side fer' many long years. Rena has be'n to school, an' has traveled, an' has had chances—better chances than anybody roun' here knows."

"She's jes' de lady I'm lookin' fer, ter teach ou' school," rejoined Wain, with emphasis. "Wid her schoolin' an' my riccommen', she kin git a fus'-class ce'tifikit an' draw fo'ty dollars a month; an' a lady er her color kin keep a lot er little niggers straighter'n a darker lady could. We jus' got ter have her ter teach ou' school—ef we kin git her."

Rena's interest in the prospect of employment at her chosen work was so great that she paid little attention to Wain's compliments. Mis' Molly led Mary B. away to the kitchen on some pretext, and left Rena to entertain the gentleman. She questioned him eagerly about the school, and he gave the most glowing accounts of the elegant schoolhouse, the bright pupils, and the congenial society of the neighborhood. He spoke almost entirely in superlatives, and, after making due allowance for what Rena perceived to be a temperamental tendency to exaggeration, she concluded that she would find in the school a worthy field of usefulness, and in this polite and good-natured though somewhat wordy man a coadjutor upon whom she could rely in her first efforts; for she was not over-confident of her powers, which seemed to grow less as the way opened for their exercise.

"Do you think I 'm competent to teach the school?" she asked of the visitor, after stating some of her qualifications.

"Oh, dere 's no doubt about it, Miss Rena," replied Wain, who had listened with an air of great wisdom, though secretly aware that he was too ignorant of letters to form a judgment; "you kin teach de school all right, an' could ef you did n't know half ez much. You won't have no trouble managin' de child'en, nuther. Ef any of 'em gits onruly, jes' call on me fer he'p, an' I'll make 'em walk Spanish. I'm chuhman er de school committee, an' I'll lam de hide off'n any scholar dat don' behave. You kin trus' me fer dat, sho' ez I'm a-settin' here."

"Then," said Rena, "I'll undertake it, and do my best. I 'm sure you'll not be too exacting."

"Yo' bes', Miss Rena, 'll be de bes' dey is. Don' you worry ner fret. Dem niggers won't have no other teacher after dey 've once laid eyes on you: I'll guarantee dat. Dere won't be no trouble, not a bit."

"Well, Cousin Molly," said Mary B. to Mis' Molly in the kitchen, "how does the plan strike you?"

"Ef Rena's satisfied, I am," replied Mis' Molly.

"But you'd better say nothin' about ketchin' a beau, or any such foolishness, er else she 'd be just as likely not to go nigh Sampson County."

"Befo' Cousin Jeff goes back," confided Mary B., "I'd like ter give 'im a party, but my house is too small. I wuz wonderin'," she added tentatively, "ef I could n' borry yo' house."

"Shorely, Ma'y B. I'm int'rested in Mr. Wain on Rena's account, an' it 's as little as I kin do to let you use my house an' help you git things ready."

The date of the party was set for Thursday night, as Wain was to leave Patesville on Friday morning, taking with him the new teacher. The party would serve the double purpose of a compliment to the guest and a farewell to Rena, and it might prove the precursor, the mother secretly hoped, of other festivities to follow at some later date.

XXII
IMPERATIVE BUSINESS

ONE Wednesday morning, about six weeks after his return home, Tryon received a letter from Judge Straight with reference to the note left with him at Patesville for collection. This communication properly required an answer, which might have been made in writing within the compass of ten lines. No sooner, however, had Tryon read the letter than he began to perceive reasons why it should be answered in person. He had left Patesville under extremely painful circumstances, vowing that he would never return; and yet now the barest pretext, by which no one could have been deceived except willingly, was sufficient to turn his footsteps thither again. He explained to his mother—with a vagueness which she found somewhat puzzling, but ascribed to her own feminine obtuseness in matters of business—the reasons that imperatively demanded his presence in Patesville. With an early start he could drive there in one day,—he had an excellent roadster, a light buggy, and a recent rain had left the road in good condition,—a day would suffice for the transaction of his business, and the third day would bring him home again. He set out on his journey on Thursday morning, with this programme very clearly outlined.

Tryon would not at first have admitted even to himself that Rena's presence in Patesville had any bearing whatever upon his projected visit. The matter about which Judge Straight had written might, it was clear, be viewed in several aspects. The judge had written him concerning the one of immediate importance. It would be much easier to discuss the subject in all its bearings, and clean up the whole matter, in one comprehensive personal interview.

The importance of this business, then, seemed very urgent for the first few hours of Tryon's journey. Ordinarily a careful driver and merciful to his beast, his eagerness to reach Patesville increased gradually until it became necessary to exercise some self-restraint in order not to urge his faithful mare beyond her powers; and soon he could no longer pretend obliviousness of the fact that some attraction stronger than the whole amount of Duncan McSwayne's note was urging him irresistibly toward his destination. The old town beyond the distant river, his heart told him clamorously, held the object in all the world to him most dear. Memory brought up in vivid detail every moment of his brief and joyous courtship,—each tender word, each enchanting smile, every fond caress. He lived his past happiness over again down to the moment of that fatal discovery. What horrible fate was it that had involved him—nay, that had caught this sweet delicate girl in such a blind alley? A wild hope flashed across his mind: perhaps the ghastly story might not be true; perhaps, after all, the girl was no more a negro than she seemed. He had heard sad stories of white children, born out of wedlock, abandoned by sinful parents to the care or adoption of colored women, who had reared them as their own, the children's future basely sacrificed to hide the parents' shame. He would confront this reputed mother of his darling and wring the truth from her. He was in a state of mind where any sort of a fairy tale would have seemed reasonable. He would almost have bribed some one to tell him that the woman he had loved, the woman he still loved (he felt a thrill of lawless pleasure in the confession), was not the descendant of slaves,—that he might marry her, and not have before his eyes the gruesome fear that some one of their children might show even the faintest mark of the despised race.

At noon he halted at a convenient hamlet, fed and watered his mare, and resumed his journey after an hour's rest. By this time he had well-nigh forgotten about the legal business that formed the ostensible occasion for his journey, and was conscious only of a wild desire to see the woman whose image was beckoning him on to Patesville as fast as his horse could take him.

At sundown he stopped again, about ten miles from the town, and cared for his now tired beast. He knew her capacity, however, and calculated that she could stand the additional ten miles without injury. The mare set out with reluctance, but soon settled resignedly down into a steady jog.

Memory had hitherto assailed Tryon with the vision of past joys. As he neared the town, imagination attacked him with still more moving images. He had left her, this sweet flower of womankind—white or not, God had never made a fairer!—he had seen her fall to the hard pavement, with he knew not what resulting injury. He had left her tender frame—the touch of her finger-tips had made him thrill with happiness—to be lifted by strange hands, while he with heartless pride had driven deliberately away, without a word of sorrow or regret. He had ignored her as completely as though she had never existed. That he had been deceived was true. But had he not aided in his own deception? Had not Warwick told him distinctly that they were of no family, and was it not his own fault that he had not followed up the clue thus given him? Had not Rena compared herself to the child's nurse, and had he not assured her that if she were the nurse, he would marry her next day? The deception had been due more to his own blindness than to any lack of honesty on the part of Rena and her brother. In the light of his present feelings they seemed to have been absurdly outspoken. He was glad that he had kept his discovery to himself. He had considered himself very magnanimous not to have exposed the fraud that was being perpetrated upon society: it was with a very comfortable feeling that he now realized that the matter was as profound a secret as before.

"She ought to have been born white," he muttered, adding weakly, "I would to God that I had never found her out!"

Drawing near the bridge that crossed the river to the town, he pictured to himself a pale girl, with sorrowful, tear-stained eyes, pining away in the old gray house behind the cedars for love of him, dying, perhaps, of a broken heart. He would hasten to her; he would dry her tears with kisses; he would express sorrow for his cruelty.

The tired mare had crossed the bridge and was slowly toiling up Front Street; she was near the limit of her endurance, and Tryon did not urge her.

They might talk the matter over, and if they must part, part at least they would in peace and friendship. If he could not marry her, he would never marry any one else; it would be cruel for him to seek happiness while she was denied it, for, having once given her heart to him, she could never, he was sure,—so instinctively fine was her nature,—she could never love any one less worthy than himself, and would therefore probably never marry. He knew from a Clarence acquaintance, who had written him a letter, that Rena had not reappeared in that town.

If he should discover—the chance was one in a thousand—that she was white; or if he should find it too hard to leave her—ah, well! he was a white man, one of a race born to command. He would make her white; no one beyond the old town would ever know the difference. If, perchance, their secret should be disclosed, the world was wide; a man of courage and ambition, inspired by love, might make a career anywhere. Circumstances made weak men; strong men mould circumstances to do their bidding. He would not let his darling die of grief, whatever the price must be paid for her salvation. She was only a few rods away from him now. In a moment he would see her; he would take her tenderly in his arms, and heart to heart they would mutually forgive and forget, and, strengthened by their love, would face the future boldly and bid the world do its worst.

XXIII
THE GUEST OF HONOR

THE evening of the party arrived. The house had been thoroughly cleaned in preparation for the event, and decorated with the choicest treasures of the garden. By eight o'clock the guests had gathered. They were all mulattoes,—all people of mixed blood were called "mulattoes" in North Carolina. There were dark mulattoes and bright mulattoes. Mis' Molly's guests were mostly of the bright class, most of them more than half white, and few of them less. In Mis' Molly's small circle, straight hair was the only palliative of a dark complexion. Many of the guests would not have been casually distinguishable from white people of the poorer class. Others bore unmistakable traces of Indian ancestry,—for Cherokee and Tuscarora blood was quite widely diffused among the free negroes of North Carolina, though well-nigh lost sight of by the curious custom of the white people to ignore anything but the negro blood in those who were touched by its potent current. Very few of those present had been slaves. The free colored people of Patesville were numerous enough before the war to have their own "society," and human enough to despise those who did not possess advantages equal to their own; and at this time they still looked down upon those who had once been held in bondage. The only black man present occupied a chair which stood on a broad chest in one corner, and extracted melody from a fiddle to which a whole generation of the best people of Patesville had danced and made merry. Uncle Needham seldom played for colored gatherings, but made an exception in Mis' Molly's case; she was not white, but he knew her past; if she was not the rose, she had at least been near the rose. When the company had gathered, Mary B., as mistress of ceremonies, whispered to Uncle Needham, who tapped his violin sharply with the bow.

"Ladies an' gent'emens, take yo' pa'dners fer a Fuhginny reel!"

Mr. Wain, as the guest of honor, opened the ball with

his hostess. He wore a broadcloth coat and trousers, a heavy glittering chain across the spacious front of his white waistcoat, and a large red rose in his buttonhole. If his boots were slightly run down at the heel, so trivial a detail passed unnoticed in the general splendor of his attire. Upon a close or hostile inspection there would have been some features of his ostensibly good-natured face—the shifty eye, the full and slightly drooping lower lip—which might have given a student of physiognomy food for reflection. But whatever the latent defects of Wain's character, he proved himself this evening a model of geniality, presuming not at all upon his reputed wealth, but winning golden opinions from those who came to criticise, of whom, of course, there were a few, the company being composed of human beings.

When the dance began, Wain extended his large, soft hand to Mary B., yellow, buxom, thirty, with white and even teeth glistening behind her full red lips. A younger sister of Mary B.'s was paired with Billy Oxendine, a funny little tailor, a great gossip, and therefore a favorite among the women. Mis' Molly graciously consented, after many protestations of lack of skill and want of practice, to stand up opposite Homer Pettifoot, Mary B.'s husband, a tall man, with a slight stoop, a bald crown, and full, dreamy eyes,—a man of much imagination and a large fund of anecdote. Two other couples completed the set; others were restrained by bashfulness or religious scruples, which did not yield until later in the evening.

The perfumed air from the garden without and the cut roses within mingled incongruously with the alien odors of musk and hair oil, of which several young barbers in the company were especially redolent. There was a play of sparkling eyes and glancing feet. Mary B. danced with the languorous grace of an Eastern odalisque, Mis' Molly with the mincing, hesitating step of one long out of practice. Wain performed saltatory prodigies. This was a golden opportunity for the display in which his soul found delight. He introduced variations hitherto unknown to the dance. His skill and suppleness brought a glow of admiration into the eyes of the women, and spread a cloud of jealousy over the faces of several of the younger men, who saw themselves eclipsed.

Rena had announced in advance her intention to take no active part in the festivities. "I don't feel like dancing, mamma—I shall never dance again."

"Well, now, Rena," answered her mother, "of co'se you 're too dignified, sence you've be'n 'sociatin' with white folks, to be hoppin' roun' an' kickin' up like Ma'y B. an' these other yaller gals; but of co'se, too, you can't slight the comp'ny entirely, even ef it ain't jest exac'ly our party,—you 'll have to pay 'em some little attention, 'specially Mr. Wain, sence you're goin' down yonder with 'im."

Rena conscientiously did what she thought politeness required. She went the round of the guests in the early part of the evening and exchanged greetings with them. To several requests for dances she replied that she was not dancing. She did not hold herself aloof because of pride; any instinctive shrinking she might have felt by reason of her recent association with persons of greater refinement was offset by her still more newly awakened zeal for humanity; they were her people, she must not despise them. But the occasion suggested painful memories of other and different scenes in which she had lately participated. Once or twice these memories were so vivid as almost to overpower her. She slipped away from the company, and kept in the background as much as possible without seeming to slight any one.

The guests as well were dimly conscious of a slight barrier between Mis' Molly's daughter and themselves. The time she had spent apart from these friends of her youth had rendered it impossible for her ever to meet them again upon the plane of common interests and common thoughts. It was much as though one, having acquired the vernacular of his native country, had lived in a foreign land long enough to lose the language of his childhood without acquiring fully that of his adopted country. Miss Rowena Warwick could never again become quite the Rena Walden who had left the house behind the cedars no more than a year and a half before. Upon this very difference were based her noble aspirations for usefulness,—one must stoop in order that one may lift others. Any other young woman present would have been importuned beyond her powers of resistance. Rena's reserve was respected.

When supper was announced, somewhat early in the evening, the dancers found seats in the hall or on the front piazza. Aunt Zilphy, assisted by Mis' Molly and Mary B., passed around the refreshments, which consisted of fried chicken, buttered biscuits, pound-cake, and eggnog. When the first edge of appetite was taken off, the conversation waxed animated. Homer Pettifoot related, with minute detail, an old, threadbare hunting lie, dating, in slightly differing forms, from the age of Nimrod, about finding twenty-five partridges sitting in a row on a rail, and killing them all with a single buckshot,

175

which passed through twenty-four and lodged in the body of the twenty-fifth, from which it was extracted and returned to the shot-pouch for future service.

This story was followed by a murmur of incredulity—of course, the thing was possible, but Homer's faculty for exaggeration was so well known that any statement of his was viewed with suspicion. Homer seemed hurt at this lack of faith, and was disposed to argue the point; but the sonorous voice of Mr. Wain on the other side of the room cut short his protestations, in much the same way that the rising sun extinguishes the light of lesser luminaries.

"I wuz a member er de fus' legislatur' after de wah," Wain was saying. "When I went up f'm Sampson in de fall, I had to pass th'ough Smithfiel'. I got in town in de afternoon, an' put up at de bes' hotel. De lan'lo'd did n' have no s'picion but what I wuz a white man, an' he gimme a room, an' I had supper an' breakfas', an' went on ter Rolly nex' mornin'. W'en de session wuz over, I come along back, an' w'en I got ter Smithfiel', I driv' up ter de same hotel. I noticed, as soon as I got dere, dat de place had run down consid'able—dere wuz weeds growin' in de yard, de winders wuz dirty, an' ev'ything roun' dere looked kinder lonesome an' shif'less. De lan'lo'd met me at de do'; he looked mighty down in de mouth, an' sezee:—

"'Look a-here, Vat made you come an' stop at my place widout tellin' me you wuz a black man? Befo' you come th'ough dis town I had a fus'-class business. But w'en folks found out dat a nigger had put up here, business drapped right off, an' I 've had ter shet up my hotel. You oughter be 'shamed er yo'se'f fer ruinin' a po' man w'at

176

had n' never done no harm ter you. You've done a mean, low-lived thing, an' a jes' God 'll punish you fer it.'

"De po' man acshully bust inter tears," continued Mr. Wain magnanimously, "an' I felt so sorry fer 'im—he wuz a po' white man tryin' ter git up in de worl'—dat I hauled out my purse an' gin 'im ten dollars, an' he 'peared monst'ous glad ter git it."

"How good-hearted! How kin'!" murmured the ladies. "It done credit to yo' feelin's."

"Don't b'lieve a word er dem lies," muttered one young man to another sarcastically. "He could n' pass fer white, 'less'n it wuz a mighty dark night."

Upon this glorious evening of his life, Mr. Jefferson Wain had one distinctly hostile critic, of whose presence he was blissfully unconscious. Frank Fowler had not been invited to the party,—his family did not go with Mary B.'s set. Rena had suggested to her mother that he be invited, but Mis' Molly had demurred on the ground that it was not her party, and that she had no right to issue invitations. It is quite likely that she would have sought an invitation for Frank from Mary B.; but Frank was black, and would not harmonize with the rest of the company, who would not have Mis' Molly's reasons for treating him well. She had compromised the matter by stepping across the way in the afternoon and suggesting that Frank might come over and sit on the back porch and look at the dancing and share in the supper.

Frank was not without a certain honest pride. He was sensitive enough, too, not to care to go where he was not wanted. He would have curtly refused any such maimed invitation to any other place. But would he not see Rena in her best attire, and might she not perhaps, in passing, speak a word to him?

"Thank y', Mis' Molly," he replied, "I 'll prob'ly come over."

"You're a big fool, boy," observed his father after Mis' Molly had gone back across the street, "ter be stickin' roun' dem yaller niggers 'cross de street, an' slobb'rin' an' slav'rin' over 'em, an' hangin' roun' deir back do' wuss 'n ef dey wuz w'ite folks. I'd see 'em dead fus'!"

Frank himself resisted the temptation for half an hour after the music began, but at length he made his way across the street and stationed himself at the window opening upon the back piazza. When Rena was in the room, he had eyes for her only, but when she was absent, he fixed his attention mainly upon Wain. With jealous clairvoyance he observed that Wain's eyes followed Rena when she left the room, and lit up when she returned. Frank had heard that Rena was going away with this man, and he watched Wain closely, liking him less the longer he looked at him. To his fancy, Wain's style and skill were affectation, his good-nature mere hypocrisy, and his glance at Rena the eye of the hawk upon his quarry. He had heard that Wain was unmarried, and he could not see how, this being so, he could help wishing Rena for a wife. Frank would have been content to see her marry a white man, who would have raised her to a plane worthy of her merits. In this man's shifty eye he read the liar—his wealth and standing were probably as false as his seeming good-humor.

"Is that you, Frank?" said a soft voice near at hand.

He looked up with a joyful thrill. Rena was peering intently at him, as if trying to distinguish his features in the darkness. It was a bright moonlight night, but Frank stood in the shadow of the piazza.

"Yas 'm, it's me, Miss Rena. Yo' mammy said I could come over an' see you-all dance. You ain' be'n out on de flo' at all, ter-night."

"No, Frank, I don't care for dancing. I shall not dance to-night."

This answer was pleasing to Frank. If he could not hope to dance with her, at least the men inside—at least this snake in the grass from down the country—should not have that privilege.

"But you must have some supper, Frank," said Rena. "I'll bring it myself."

"No, Miss Rena, I don' keer fer nothin'—I did n' come over ter eat—r'al'y I did n't."

"Nonsense, Frank, there 's plenty of it. I have no appetite, and you shall have my portion."

She brought him a slice of cake and a glass of eggnog. When Mis' Molly, a minute later, came out upon the piazza, Frank left the yard and walked down the street toward the old canal. Rena had spoken softly to him; she had fed him with her own dainty hands. He might never hope that she would see in him anything but a friend; but he loved her, and he would watch over her and protect her, wherever she might be. He did not believe that she would ever marry the grinning hypocrite masquerading back there in Mis' Molly's parlor; but the man would bear watching.

Mis' Molly had come to call her daughter into the house. "Rena," she said, "Mr. Wain wants ter know if you won't dance just one dance with him."

"Yas, Rena," pleaded Mary B., who followed Miss Molly out to the piazza, "jes' one dance. I don't think you're treatin' my comp'ny jes' right, Cousin Rena."

"You're goin' down there with 'im," added her mother, "an' it'd be just as well to be on friendly terms with 'im."

Wain himself had followed the women. "Sho'ly, Miss Rena, you're gwine ter honah me wid one dance? I'd go 'way f'm dis pa'ty sad at hea't ef I had n' stood up oncet wid de young lady er de house."

As Rena, weakly persuaded, placed her hand on Wain's arm and entered the house, a buggy, coming up Front Street, paused a moment at the corner, and then turning slowly, drove quietly up the nameless by-street, concealed by the intervening cedars, until it reached a point from which the occupant could view, through the open front window, the interior of the parlor.

XXIV
SWING YOUR PARTNERS

MOVED by tenderness and thoughts of self-sacrifice, which had occupied his mind to the momentary exclusion of all else, Tryon had scarcely noticed, as he approached the house behind the cedars, a strain of lively music, to which was added, as he drew still nearer, the accompaniment of other festive sounds. He suddenly awoke, however, to the fact that these signs of merriment came from the house at which he had intended to stop;— he had not meant that Rena should pass another sleepless night of sorrow, or that he should himself endure another needless hour of suspense.

He drew rein at the corner. Shocked surprise, a nascent anger, a vague alarm, an insistent curiosity, urged him nearer. Turning the mare into the side street and keeping close to the fence, he drove ahead in the shadow of the cedars until he reached a gap through which he could see into the open door and windows of the brightly lighted hall.

There was evidently a ball in progress. The fiddle was squeaking merrily to a tune that he remembered well,— it was associated with one of the most delightful evenings of his life, that of the tournament ball. A mellow negro voice was calling with a rhyming accompaniment the figures of a quadrille. Tryon, with parted lips and slowly hardening heart, leaned forward from the buggy-seat, gripping the rein so tightly that his nails cut into the opposing palm. Above the clatter of noisy conversation rose the fiddler's voice:—

> "Swing yo' pa'dners; doan be shy,
> Look yo' lady in de eye!
> Th'ow yo' ahm aroun' huh wais';
> Take yo' time—dey ain' no has'e!"

To the middle of the floor, in full view through an open window, advanced the woman who all day long had been the burden of his thoughts—not pale with grief and hollow-eyed with weeping, but flushed with pleasure, around her waist the arm of a burly, grinning mulatto, whose face was offensively familiar to Tryon.

With a muttered curse of concentrated bitterness, Tryon struck the mare a sharp blow with the whip. The sensitive creature, spirited even in her great weariness, resented the lash and started off with the bit in her teeth. Perceiving that it would be difficult to turn in the nar-

181

row roadway without running into the ditch at the left, Tryon gave the mare rein and dashed down the street, scarcely missing, as the buggy crossed the bridge, a man standing abstractedly by the old canal, who sprang aside barely in time to avoid being run over.

Meantime Rena was passing through a trying ordeal. After the first few bars, the fiddler plunged into a well-known air, in which Rena, keenly susceptible to musical impressions, recognized the tune to which, as Queen of Love and Beauty, she had opened the dance at her entrance into the world of life and love, for it was there she had met George Tryon. The combination of music and movement brought up the scene with great distinctness. Tryon, peering angrily through the cedars, had not been more conscious than she of the external contrast between her partners on this and the former occasion. She perceived, too, as Tryon from the outside had not, the difference between Wain's wordy flattery (only saved by his cousin's warning from pointed and fulsome adulation), and the tenderly graceful compliment, couched in the romantic terms of chivalry, with which the knight of the handkerchief had charmed her ear. It was only by an immense effort that she was able to keep her emotions under control until the end of the dance, when she fled to her chamber and burst into tears. It was not the cruel Tryon who had blasted her love with his deadly look that she mourned, but the gallant young knight who had worn her favor on his lance and crowned her Queen of Love and Beauty.

Tryon's stay in Patesville was very brief. He drove to the hotel and put up for the night. During many sleepless hours his mind was in a turmoil with a very different set of thoughts from those which had occupied it on the way to town. Not the least of them was a profound self-contempt for his own lack of discernment. How had he been so blind as not to have read long ago the character of this wretched girl who had bewitched him? To-night his eyes had been opened—he had seen her with the mask thrown off, a true daughter of a race in which the sensuous enjoyment of the moment took precedence of taste or sentiment or any of the higher emotions. Her few months of boarding-school, her brief association with white people, had evidently been a mere veneer over the underlying negro, and their effects had slipped away as soon as the intercourse had ceased. With the monkey-like imitativeness of the negro she had copied the manners of white people while she lived among them, and had dropped them with equal facility when they ceased to serve a purpose. Who but a negro could have recovered so soon from what had seemed a terrible bereavement?—she herself must have felt it at the time, for otherwise she would not have swooned. A woman of sensibility, as this one had seemed to be, should naturally feel more keenly, and for a longer time than a man, an injury to the affections; but he, a son of the ruling race, had been miserable for six weeks about a girl who had so far forgotten him as already to plunge headlong into the childish amusements of her own ignorant and degraded people. What more, indeed, he asked himself savagely,—what more could be expected of the base-born child of the plaything of a gentleman's idle hour, who to this ignoble origin added the blood of a servile race? And he, George Tryon, had honored her with his love; he had very nearly linked his fate and joined his blood to hers by the solemn sanctions of church and state. Tryon was not a devout man, but he thanked God with religious fervor that he had been saved a second time from a mistake which would have wrecked his whole future. If he had yielded to the momentary weakness of the past night,—the outcome of a sickly sentimentality to which he recognized now, in the light of reflection, that he was entirely too prone,—he would have regretted it soon enough. The black streak would have been sure to come out in some form, sooner or later, if not in the wife, then in her children. He saw clearly enough, in this hour of revulsion, that with his temperament and training such a union could never have been happy. If all the world had been ignorant of the dark secret, it would always have been in his own thoughts, or at least never far away. Each fault of hers that the close daily association of husband and wife might reveal,—the most flawless of sweethearts do not pass scathless through the long test of matrimony,—every wayward impulse of his children, every defect of mind, morals, temper, or health, would have been ascribed to the dark ancestral strain. Happiness under such conditions would have been impossible.

When Tryon lay awake in the early morning, after a few brief hours of sleep, the business which had brought him to Patesville seemed, in the cold light of reason, so ridiculously inadequate that he felt almost ashamed to have set up such a pretext for his journey. The prospect, too, of meeting Dr. Green and his family, of having to explain his former sudden departure, and of running a gauntlet of inquiry concerning his marriage to the aristocratic Miss Warwick of South Carolina; the fear that some one at Patesville might have suspected a connection between Rena's swoon and his own flight,—these considerations so moved this impressionable and impulsive young man that he called a bell-boy, demanded an early breakfast, ordered his horse, paid his reckoning, and started upon his homeward journey forthwith. A certain distrust of his own sensibility, which he felt to be curiously inconsistent with his most positive convictions, led him to seek the river bridge by a roundabout route which did not take him past the house where, a few hours before, he had seen the last fragment of his idol shattered beyond the hope of repair.

The party broke up at an early hour, since most of the guests were working-people, and the travelers were to make an early start next day. About nine in the morning, Wain drove round to Mis' Molly's. Rena's trunk was strapped behind the buggy, and she set out, in the company of Wain, for her new field of labor. The school term was only two months in length, and she did not expect to return until its expiration. Just before taking her seat in the buggy, Rena felt a sudden sinking of the heart.

"Oh, mother," she whispered, as they stood wrapped in a close embrace, "I 'm afraid to leave you. I left you once, and it turned out so miserably."

"It 'll turn out better this time, honey," replied her mother soothingly. "Good-by, child. Take care of yo'self an' yo'r money, and write to yo'r mammy."

One kiss all round, and Rena was lifted into the buggy. Wain seized the reins, and under his skillful touch the pretty mare began to prance and curvet with restrained impatience. Wain could not resist the opportunity to show off before the party, which included Mary B.'s entire family and several other neighbors, who had gathered to see the travelers off.

"Good-by ter Patesville! Good-by, folkses all!" he cried, with a wave of his disengaged hand.

"Good-by, mother! Good-by, all!" cried Rena, as with tears in her heart and a brave smile on her face she left her home behind her for the second time.

When they had crossed the river bridge, the travelers came to a long stretch of rising ground, from the summit of which they could look back over the white sandy road for nearly a mile. Neither Rena nor her companion saw Frank Fowler behind the chinquapin bush at the foot of the hill, nor the gaze of mute love and longing with which he watched the buggy mount the long incline. He had not been able to trust himself to bid her farewell. He had seen her go away once before with every prospect of happiness, and come back, a dove with a wounded wing, to the old nest behind the cedars. She was going away again, with a man whom he disliked and distrusted. If she had met misfortune before, what were her prospects for happiness now?

The buggy paused at the top of the hill, and Frank, shading his eyes with his hand, thought he could see her turn and look behind. Look back, dear child, towards your home and those who love you! For who knows more than this faithful worshiper what threads of the past Fate is weaving into your future, or whether happiness or misery lies before you?

XXV
BALANCE ALL

THE road to Sampson County lay for the most part over the pine-clad sandhills,—an alternation of gentle rises and gradual descents, with now and then a swamp of greater or less extent. Long stretches of the highway led through the virgin forest, for miles unbroken by a clearing or sign of human habitation.

They traveled slowly, with frequent pauses in shady places, for the weather was hot. The journey, made leisurely, required more than a day, and might with slight effort be prolonged into two. They stopped for the night at a small village, where Wain found lodging for Rena with an acquaintance of his, and for himself with another, while a third took charge of the horse, the accommodation for travelers being limited. Rena's appearance and manners were the subject of much comment. It was necessary to explain to several curious white people that Rena was a woman of color. A white woman might have driven with Wain without attracting remark,—most white ladies had negro coachmen. That a woman of Rena's complexion should eat at a negro's table, or sleep beneath a negro's roof, was a seeming breach of caste which only black blood could excuse. The explanation was never questioned. No white person of sound mind would ever claim to be a negro.

They resumed their journey somewhat late in the morning. Rena would willingly have hastened, for she was anxious to plunge into her new work; but Wain seemed disposed to prolong the pleasant drive, and beguiled the way for a time with stories of wonderful things he had done and strange experiences of a somewhat checkered career. He was shrewd enough to avoid any subject which would offend a modest young woman, but too obtuse to perceive that much of what he said would not commend him to a person of refinement. He made little reference to his possessions, concerning which so much had been said at Patesville; and this reticence was a point in his favor. If he had not been so much upon his guard and Rena so much absorbed by thoughts of her future work, such a drive would have furnished a person of her discernment a very fair measure of the man's character. To these distractions must be added the entire absence of any idea that Wain might have amorous designs upon her; and any shortcomings of manners or speech were excused by the broad mantle of charity which Rena in her new-found zeal for the welfare of her people was willing to throw over all their faults. They were the victims of oppression; they were not responsible for its results.

Toward the end of the second day, while nearing their destination, the travelers passed a large white house standing back from the road at the foot of a lane. Around it grew widespreading trees and well-kept shrubbery. The fences were in good repair. Behind the house and across the road stretched extensive fields of cotton and waving corn. They had passed no other place that showed such signs of thrift and prosperity.

"Oh, what a lovely place!" exclaimed Rena. "That is yours, is n't it?"

"No; we ain't got to my house yet," he answered. "Dat house b'longs ter de riches' people roun' here. Dat house is over in de nex' county. We're right close to de line now."

Shortly afterwards they turned off from the main highway they had been pursuing, and struck into a narrower road to the left.

"De main road," explained Wain, "goes on to Clinton, 'bout five miles er mo' away. Dis one we're turnin' inter now will take us to my place, which is 'bout three miles fu'ther on. We'll git dere now in an hour er so."

Wain lived in an old plantation house, somewhat dilapidated, and surrounded by an air of neglect and shiftlessness, but still preserving a remnant of dignity in its outlines and comfort in its interior arrangements. Rena was assigned a large room on the second floor. She was somewhat surprised at the make-up of the household. Wain's mother—an old woman, much darker than her son—kept house for him. A sister with two children lived in the house. The element of surprise lay in the presence of two small children left by Wain's wife, of whom Rena now heard for the first time. He had lost his wife, he informed Rena sadly, a couple of years before.

"Yas, Miss Rena," she sighed, "de Lawd give her, an' de Lawd tuck her away. Blessed be de name er de Lawd." He accompanied this sententious quotation with a wicked look from under his half-closed eyelids that Rena did not see.

The following morning Wain drove her in his buggy over to the county town, where she took the teacher's examination. She was given a seat in a room with a number of other candidates for certificates, but the fact leaking out from some remark of Wain's that she was a colored girl, objection was quietly made by several of the would-be teachers to her presence in the room, and she was requested to retire until the white teachers should have been examined. An hour or two later she was given a separate examination, which she passed without difficulty. The examiner, a gentleman of local standing, was dimly conscious that she might not have found her exclusion pleasant, and was especially polite. It would have been strange, indeed, if he had not been impressed by her sweet face and air of modest dignity, which were all the more striking because of her social disability. He fell into conversation with her, became interested in her hopes and aims, and very cordially offered to be of service, if at any time he might, in connection with her school.

"You have the satisfaction," he said, "of receiving the only first-grade certificate issued to-day. You might teach a higher grade of pupils than you will find at Sandy Run, but let us hope that you may in time raise them to your own level."

"Which I doubt very much," he muttered to himself, as she went away with Wain. "What a pity that such a woman should be a nigger! If she were anything to me, though, I should hate to trust her anywhere near that saddle-colored scoundrel. He's a thoroughly bad lot, and will bear watching."

Rena, however, was serenely ignorant of any danger from the accommodating Wain. Absorbed in her own thoughts and plans, she had not sought to look beneath the surface of his somewhat overdone politeness. In a few days she began her work as teacher, and sought to forget in the service of others the dull sorrow that still gnawed at her heart.

XXVI
THE SCHOOLHOUSE IN THE WOODS

BLANCHE LEARY, closely observant of Tryon's moods, marked a decided change in his manner after his return from his trip to Patesville. His former moroseness had given way to a certain defiant lightness, broken now and then by an involuntary sigh, but maintained so well, on the whole, that his mother detected no lapses whatever. The change was characterized by another feature agreeable to both the women: Tryon showed decidedly more interest than ever before in Miss Leary's society. Within a week he asked her several times to play a selection on the piano, displaying, as she noticed, a decided preference for gay and cheerful music, and several times suggesting a change when she chose pieces of a sentimental cast. More than once, during the second week after his return, he went out riding with her; she was a graceful horsewoman, perfectly at home in the saddle, and appearing to advantage in a riding-habit. She was aware that Tryon watched her now and then, with an eye rather critical than indulgent.

"He is comparing me with some other girl," she surmised. "I seem to stand the test very well. I wonder who the other is, and what was the trouble?"

Miss Leary exerted all her powers to interest and amuse the man she had set out to win, and who seemed nearer than ever before. Tryon, to his pleased surprise, discovered in her mind depths that he had never suspected. She displayed a singular affinity for the tastes that were his—he could not, of course, know how carefully she had studied them. The old wound, recently re-opened, seemed to be healing rapidly, under conditions more conducive than before to perfect recovery. No longer, indeed, was he pursued by the picture of Rena discovered and unmasked—this he had definitely banished from the realm of sentiment to that of reason. The haunting image of Rena loving and beloved, amid the harmonious surroundings of her brother's home, was not so readily displaced. Nevertheless, he reached in several weeks a point from which he could consider her as one thinks of a dear one removed by the hand of death, or smitten by some incurable ailment of mind or body. Erelong, he fondly believed, the recovery would be so far complete that he could consign to the tomb of pleasant memories even the most thrilling episodes of his ill-starred courtship.

"George," said Mrs. Tryon one morning while her son was in this cheerful mood, "I 'm sending Blanche over to Major McLeod's to do an errand for me. Would you mind driving her over? The road may be rough after the storm last night, and Blanche has an idea that no one drives so well as you."

"Why, yes, mother, I'll be glad to drive Blanche over. I want to see the major myself."

They were soon bowling along between the pines, behind the handsome mare that had carried Tryon so well at the Clarence tournament. Presently he drew up sharply.

"A tree has fallen squarely across the road," he exclaimed. "We shall have to turn back a little way and go around."

They drove back a quarter of a mile and turned into a by-road leading to the right through the woods. The solemn silence of the pine forest is soothing or oppressive, according to one's mood. Beneath the cool arcade of the tall, overarching trees a deep peace stole over Tryon's heart. He had put aside indefinitely and forever an unhappy and impossible love. The pretty and affectionate girl beside him would make an ideal wife. Of her family and blood he was sure. She was his mother's choice, and his mother had set her heart upon their marriage. Why not speak to her now, and thus give himself the best possible protection against stray flames of love?

"Blanche," he said, looking at her kindly.

"Yes, George?" Her voice was very gentle, and slightly tremulous. Could she have divined his thought? Love is a great clairvoyant.

"Blanche, dear, I"—

A clatter of voices broke upon the stillness of the forest and interrupted Tryon's speech. A sudden turn to the left brought the buggy to a little clearing, in the midst of which stood a small log schoolhouse. Out of the schoolhouse a swarm of colored children were emerging, the suppressed energy of the school hour finding vent in vocal exercise of various sorts. A group had already formed a ring, and were singing with great volume and vigor:—

> "Miss Jane, she loves sugar an' tea,
> Miss Jane, she loves candy.
> Miss Jane, she can whirl all around
> An' kiss her love quite handy.

> "De oak grows tall,
> De pine grows slim,
> So rise you up, my true love,
> An' let me come in."

"What a funny little darkey!" exclaimed Miss Leary, pointing to a diminutive lad who was walking on his hands, with his feet balanced in the air. At sight of the buggy and its occupants this sable acrobat, still retaining his inverted position, moved toward the newcomers, and, reversing himself with a sudden spring, brought up standing beside the buggy.

"Hoddy, Mars Geo'ge!" he exclaimed, bobbing his head and kicking his heel out behind in approved plantation style.

"Hello, Plato," replied the young man, "what are you doing here?"

"Gwine ter school, Mars Geo'ge," replied the lad; "larnin' ter read an' write, suh, lack de w'ite folks."

"Wat you callin' dat w'ite man marster fur?" whispered a tall yellow boy to the acrobat addressed as Plato. "You don' b'long ter him no mo'; you're free, an' ain' got sense ernuff ter know it."

Tryon threw a small coin to Plato, and holding another in his hand suggestively, smiled toward the tall yellow boy, who looked regretfully at the coin, but stood his ground; he would call no man master, not even for a piece of money.

During this little colloquy, Miss Leary had kept her face turned toward the schoolhouse.

"What a pretty girl!" she exclaimed. "There," she added, as Tryon turned his head toward her, "you are too late. She has retired into her castle. Oh, Plato!"

"Yas, missis," replied Plato, who was prancing round the buggy in great glee, on the strength of his acquaintance with the white folks.

"Is your teacher white?"

"No, ma'm, she ain't w'ite; she 's black. She looks lack she's w 'ite, but she 's black."

Tryon had not seen the teacher's face, but the incident had jarred the old wound; Miss Leary's description of the teacher, together with Plato's characterization, had stirred lightly sleeping memories. He was more or less abstracted during the remainder of the drive, and did not recur to the conversation that had been interrupted by coming upon the schoolhouse.

The teacher, glancing for a moment through the open door of the schoolhouse, had seen a handsome young lady staring at her,—Miss Leary had a curiously intent look when she was interested in anything, with no intention whatever to be rude,—and beyond the lady the back and shoulder of a man, whose face was turned the other way. There was a vague suggestion of something familiar about the equipage, but Rena shrank from this close scrutiny and withdrew out of sight before she had had an opportunity to identify the vague resemblance to something she had known.

Miss Leary had missed by a hair's-breadth the psychological moment, and felt some resentment toward the little negroes who had interrupted her lover's train of thought. Negroes have caused a great deal of trouble among white people. How deeply the shadow of the Ethiopian had fallen upon her own happiness, Miss Leary of course could not guess.

XXVII
AN INTERESTING ACQUAINTANCE

A FEW days later, Rena looked out of the window near her desk and saw a low basket phaeton, drawn by a sorrel pony, driven sharply into the clearing and drawn up beside an oak sapling. The occupant of the phaeton, a tall, handsome, well-preserved lady in middle life, with slightly gray hair, alighted briskly from the phaeton, tied the pony to the sapling with a hitching-strap, and advanced to the schoolhouse door.

Rena wondered who the lady might be. She had a benevolent aspect, however, and came forward to the desk with a smile, not at all embarrassed by the wide-eyed inspection of the entire school.

"How do you do?" she said, extending her hand to the teacher. "I live in the neighborhood and am interested in the colored people—a good many of them once belonged to me. I heard something of your school, and thought I should like to make your acquaintance."

"It is very kind of you, indeed," murmured Rena respectfully.

"Yes," continued the lady, "I am not one of those who sit back and blame their former slaves because they were freed. They are free now,—it is all decided and settled,—and they ought to be taught enough to enable them to make good use of their freedom. But really, my dear,—you must n't feel offended if I make a mistake,—I am going to ask you something very personal." She looked suggestively at the gaping pupils.

"The school may take the morning recess now," announced the teacher. The pupils filed out in an orderly manner, most of them stationing themselves about the grounds in such places as would keep the teacher and the white lady in view. Very few white persons approved of the colored schools; no other white person had ever visited this one.

"Are you really colored?" asked the lady, when the children had withdrawn.

A year and a half earlier, Rena would have met the question by some display of self-consciousness. Now, she replied simply and directly.

"Yes, ma'am, I am colored."

The lady, who had been studying her as closely as good manners would permit, sighed regretfully.

"Well, it's a shame. No one would ever think it. If you chose to conceal it, no one would ever be the wiser. What is your name, child, and where were you brought up? You must have a romantic history."

Rena gave her name and a few facts in regard to her past. The lady was so much interested, and put so many and such searching questions, that Rena really found it more difficult to suppress the fact that she had been white, than she had formerly had in hiding her African origin. There was about the girl an air of real refinement that pleased the lady,—the refinement not merely of a fine nature, but of contact with cultured people; a certain reserve of speech and manner quite inconsistent with Mrs. Tryon's experience of colored women. The lady was interested and slightly mystified. A generous, impulsive spirit,—her son's own mother,—she made minute inquiries about the school and the pupils, several of whom she knew by name. Rena stated that the two months' term was nearing its end, and that she was training the children in various declamations and dialogues for the exhibition at the close.

"I shall attend it," declared the lady positively. "I'm sure you are doing a good work, and it 's very noble of you to undertake it when you might have a very different future. If I can serve you at any time, don't hesitate to call upon me. I live in the big white house just before you turn out of the Clinton road to come this way. I'm only a widow, but my son George lives with me and has some influence in the neighborhood. He drove by here yesterday with the lady he is going to marry. It was she who told me about you."

Was it the name, or some subtle resemblance in speech or feature, that recalled Tryon's image to Rena's mind? It was not so far away—the image of the loving Tryon—that any powerful witchcraft was required to call it up. His mother was a widow; Rena had thought, in happier days, that she might be such a kind lady as this. But the cruel Tryon who had left her—his mother would be some hard, cold, proud woman, who would regard a negro as but little better than a dog, and who would not soil her lips by addressing a colored person upon any other terms than as a servant. She knew, too, that Tryon did not live in Sampson County, though the exact location of his home was not clear to her.

"And where are you staying, my dear?" asked the good lady.

"I'm boarding at Mrs. Wain's," answered Rena.

"Mrs. Wain's?"

"Yes, they live in the old Campbell place."

"Oh, yes—Aunt Nancy. She 's a good enough woman, but we don't think much of her son Jeff. He married my

Amanda after the war—she used to belong to me, and ought to have known better. He abused her most shamefully, and had to be threatened with the law. She left him a year or so ago and went away; I have n't seen her lately. Well, good-by, child; I'm coming to your exhibition. If you ever pass my house, come in and see me."

The good lady had talked for half an hour, and had brought a ray of sunshine into the teacher's monotonous life, heretofore lighted only by the uncertain lamp of high resolve. She had satisfied a pardonable curiosity, and had gone away without mentioning her name.

Rena saw Plato untying the pony as the lady climbed into the phaeton.

"Who was the lady, Plato?" asked the teacher when the visitor had driven away.

"Dat 'uz my ole mist'iss, ma'm," returned Plato proudly,—"ole Mis' 'Liza."

"Mis' 'Liza who?" asked Rena.

"Mis' 'Liza Tryon. I use' ter b'long ter her. Dat 'uz her son, my young Mars Geo'ge, w'at driv pas' hyuh yistiddy wid 'is sweetheart."

XXVIII
THE LOST KNIFE

RENA had found her task not a difficult one so far as discipline was concerned. Her pupils were of a docile race, and school to them had all the charm of novelty. The teacher commanded some awe because she was a stranger, and some, perhaps, because she was white; for the theory of blackness as propounded by Plato could not quite counterbalance in the young African mind the evidence of their own senses. She combined gentleness with firmness; and if these had not been sufficient, she had reserves of character which would have given her the mastery over much less plastic material than these ignorant but eager young people. The work of instruction was simple enough, for most of the pupils began with the alphabet, which they acquired from Webster's blue-backed spelling-book, the palladium of Southern education at that epoch. The much abused carpet-baggers had put the spelling-book within reach of every child of school age in North Carolina,—a fact which is often overlooked when the carpet-baggers are held up to public odium. Even the devil should have his due, and is not so black as he is painted.

At the time when she learned that Tryon lived in the neighborhood, Rena had already been subjected for several weeks to a trying ordeal. Wain had begun to persecute her with marked attentions. She had at first gone to board at his house,—or, by courtesy, with his mother. For a week or two she had considered his attentions in no other light than those of a member of the school committee sharing her own zeal and interested in seeing the school successfully carried on. In this character Wain had driven her to the town for her examination; he had busied himself about putting the schoolhouse in order, and in various matters affecting the conduct of the school. He had jocularly offered to come and whip the children for her, and had found it convenient to drop in occasionally, ostensibly to see what progress the work was making.

"Dese child'en," he would observe sonorously, in the presence of the school, "oughter be monst'ous glad ter have de chance er settin' under yo' instruction, Miss Rena. I'm sho' eve'body in dis neighbo'hood 'preciates de priv'lege er havin' you in ou' mids'."

Though slightly embarrassing to the teacher, these public demonstrations were endurable so long as they could be regarded as mere official appreciation of her work. Sincerely in earnest about her undertaking, she had plunged into it with all the intensity of a serious nature which love had stirred to activity. A pessimist might have sighed sadly or smiled cynically at the notion that a poor, weak girl, with a dangerous beauty and a sensitive soul, and troubles enough of her own, should hope to accomplish anything appreciable toward lifting the black mass still floundering in the mud where slavery had left it, and where emancipation had found it,—the mud in which, for aught that could be seen to the contrary, her little feet, too, were hopelessly entangled. It might have seemed like expecting a man to lift himself by his boot-straps.

But Rena was no philosopher, either sad or cheerful. She could not even have replied to this argument, that races must lift themselves, and the most that can be done by others is to give them opportunity and fair play. Hers was a simpler reasoning,—the logic by which the world is kept going onward and upward when philosophers are at odds and reformers are not forthcoming. She knew that for every child she taught to read and write she opened, if ever so little, the door of opportunity, and she was happy in the consciousness of performing a duty which seemed all the more imperative because newly discovered. Her zeal, indeed, for the time being was like that of an early Christian, who was more willing than not to die for his faith. Rena had fully and firmly made up her mind to sacrifice her life upon this altar. Her absorption in the work had not been without its reward, for thereby she had been able to keep at a distance the spectre of her lost love. Her dreams she could not control, but she banished Tryon as far as possible from her waking thoughts.

When Wain's attentions became obviously personal, Rena's new vestal instinct took alarm, and she began to apprehend his character more clearly. She had long ago learned that his pretensions to wealth were a sham. He was nominal owner of a large plantation, it is true; but the land was worn out, and mortgaged to the limit of its security value. His reputed droves of cattle and hogs had dwindled to a mere handful of lean and listless brutes.

Her clear eye, when once set to take Wain's measure, soon fathomed his shallow, selfish soul, and detected, or at least divined, behind his mask of good-nature a lurking brutality which filled her with vague distrust, needing only occasion to develop it into active apprehension,—occasion which was not long wanting. She avoided being alone with him at home by keeping carefully with the women of the house. If she were left alone,—and they soon showed a tendency to leave her on any pretext whenever Wain came near,—she would seek her own room and lock the door. She preferred not to offend Wain; she was far away from home and in a measure in his power, but she dreaded his compliments and sickened at his smile. She was also compelled to hear his relations sing his praises.

"My son Jeff," old Mrs. Wain would say, "is de bes' man you ever seed. His fus' wife had de easies' time an' de happies' time er ary woman in dis settlement. He's grieve' fer her a long time, but I reckon he 's gittin' over it, an' de nex' 'oman w'at marries him 'll git a box er pyo' gol', ef I does say it as is his own mammy."

Rena had thought Wain rather harsh with his household, except in her immediate presence. His mother and sister seemed more or less afraid of him, and the children often anxious to avoid him.

One day, he timed his visit to the schoolhouse so as to walk home with Rena through the woods. When she became aware of his purpose, she called to one of the children who was loitering behind the others, "Wait a minute, Jenny. I 'm going your way, and you can walk along with me."

Wain with difficulty hid a scowl behind a smiling front. When they had gone a little distance along the road through the woods, he clapped his hand upon his pocket.

"I declare ter goodness," he exclaimed, "ef I ain't dropped my pocket-knife! I thought I felt somethin' slip th'ough dat hole in my pocket jes' by the big pine stump in the schoolhouse ya'd. Jinny, chile, run back an' hunt fer my knife, an' I 'll give yer five cents ef yer find it. Me an' Miss Rena 'll walk on slow 'tel you ketches us."

Rena did not dare to object, though she was afraid to be alone with this man. If she could have had a moment to think, she would have volunteered to go back with Jenny and look for the knife, which, although a palpable subterfuge on her part, would have been one to which Wain could not object; but the child, dazzled by the prospect of reward, had darted back so quickly that this way of escape was cut off. She was evidently in for a declaration of love, which she had taken infinite pains to avoid. Just the form it would assume, she could not foresee. She was not long left in suspense. No sooner was the child well out of sight than Wain threw his arms suddenly about her waist and smiling, attempted to kiss her.

Speechless with fear and indignation, she tore herself from his grasp with totally unexpected force, and fled incontinently along the forest path. Wain—who, to do him justice, had merely meant to declare his passion in what he had hoped might prove a not unacceptable fashion—followed in some alarm, expostulating and apologizing as he went. But he was heavy and Rena was light, and fear lent wings to her feet. He followed her until he saw her enter the house of Elder Johnson, the father of several of her pupils, after which he sneaked uneasily homeward, somewhat apprehensive of the consequences of his abrupt wooing, which was evidently open to an unfavorable construction. When, an hour later, Rena sent one of the Johnson children for some of her things, with a message explaining that the teacher had been invited to spend a few days at Elder Johnson's, Wain felt a pronounced measure of relief. For an hour he had even thought it might be better to relinquish his pursuit. With a fatuousness born of vanity, however, no sooner had she sent her excuse than he began to look upon her visit to Johnson's as a mere exhibition of coyness, which, together with her conduct in the woods, was merely intended to lure him on.

Right upon the heels of the perturbation caused by Wain's conduct, Rena discovered that Tryon lived in the neighborhood; that not only might she meet him any day upon the highway, but that he had actually driven by the schoolhouse. That he knew or would know of her proximity there could be no possible doubt, since she had freely told his mother her name and her home. A hot wave of shame swept over her at the thought that George Tryon might imagine she were following him, throwing herself in his way, and at the thought of the construction which he might place upon her actions. Caught thus between two emotional fires, at the very time when her school duties, owing to the approaching exhibition, demanded all her energies, Rena was subjected to a physical and mental strain that only youth and health could have resisted, and then only for a short time.

XXIX
PLATO EARNS HALF A DOLLAR

Tryon's first feeling, when his mother at the dinner-table gave an account of her visit to the schoolhouse in the woods, was one of extreme annoyance. Why, of all created beings, should this particular woman be chosen to teach the colored school at Sandy Run? Had she learned that he lived in the neighborhood, and had she sought the place hoping that he might consent to renew, on different terms, relations which could never be resumed upon their former footing? Six weeks before, he would not have believed her capable of following him; but his last visit to Patesville had revealed her character in such a light that it was difficult to predict what she might do.

It was, however, no affair of his. He was done with her; he had dismissed her from his own life, where she had never properly belonged, and he had filled her place, or would soon fill it, with another and worthier woman. Even his mother, a woman of keen discernment and delicate intuitions, had been deceived by this girl's specious exterior. She had brought away from her interview of the morning the impression that Rena was a fine, pure spirit, born out of place, through some freak of Fate, devoting herself with heroic self-sacrifice to a noble cause. Well, he had imagined her just as pure and fine, and she had deliberately, with a negro's low cunning, deceived him into believing that she was a white girl. The pretended confession of the brother, in which he had spoken of the humble origin of the family, had been, consciously or unconsciously, the most disingenuous feature of the whole miserable performance. They had tried by a show of frankness to satisfy their own consciences,—they doubtless had enough of white blood to give them a rudimentary trace of such a moral organ,—and by the same act to disarm him against future recriminations, in the event of possible discovery. How was he to imagine that persons of their appearance and pretensions were tainted with negro blood? The more he dwelt upon the subject, the more angry he became with those who had surprised his virgin heart and deflowered it by such low trickery. The man who brought the first negro into the British colonies had committed a crime against humanity and a worse crime against his own race. The father of this girl had been guilty of a sin against society for which others— for which he, George Tryon—must pay the penalty. As slaves, negroes were tolerable. As freemen, they were an excrescence, an alien element incapable of absorption into the body politic of white men. He would like to send them all back to the Africa from which their forefathers had come,—unwillingly enough, he would admit,—and he would like especially to banish this girl from his own neighborhood; not indeed that her presence would make any difference to him, except as a humiliating reminder of his own folly and weakness with which he could very well dispense.

Of this state of mind Tryon gave no visible manifestation beyond a certain taciturnity, so much at variance with his recent liveliness that the ladies could not fail to notice it. No effort upon the part of either was able to affect his mood, and they both resigned themselves to await his lordship's pleasure to be companionable.

For a day or two, Tryon sedulously kept away from the neighborhood of the schoolhouse at Sandy Run. He really had business which would have taken him in that direction, but made a détour of five miles rather than go near his abandoned and discredited sweetheart.

But George Tryon was wisely distrustful of his own impulses. Driving one day along the road to Clinton, he overhauled a diminutive black figure trudging along the road, occasionally turning a handspring by way of diversion.

"Hello, Plato," called Tryon, "do you want a lift?"

"Hoddy, Mars Geo'ge. Kin I ride wid you?"

"Jump up."

Plato mounted into the buggy with the agility to be expected from a lad of his acrobatic accomplishments. The two almost immediately fell into conversation upon perhaps the only subject of common interest between them. Before the town was reached, Tryon knew, so far as Plato could make it plain, the estimation in which the teacher was held by pupils and parents. He had learned the hours of opening and dismissal of the school, where the teacher lived, her habits of coming to and going from the schoolhouse, and the road she always followed.

"Does she go to church or anywhere else with Jeff Wain, Plato?" asked Tryon.

"No, suh, she don' go nowhar wid nobody excep'n' ole Elder Johnson er Mis' Johnson, an' de child'en. She use' ter stop at Mis' Wain's, but she's stayin' wid Elder Johnson now. She alluz makes some er de child'en go home wid er f'm school," said Plato, proud to find in Mars Geo'ge an appreciative listener,—"sometimes one an' sometimes anudder. I's be'n home wid 'er twice, an' it'll be my tu'n ag'in befo' long."

"Plato," remarked Tryon impressively, as they drove into the town, "do you think you could keep a secret?"

"Yas, Mars Geo'ge, ef you says I shill."

"Do you see this fifty-cent piece?" Tryon displayed a small piece of paper money, crisp and green in its newness.

"Yas, Mars Geo'ge," replied Plato, fixing his eyes respectfully on the government's promise to pay. Fifty cents was a large sum of money. His acquaintance with Mars Geo'ge gave him the privilege of looking at money. When he grew up, he would be able, in good times, to earn fifty cents a day.

"I am going to give this to you, Plato."

Plato's eyes opened wide as saucers. "Me, Mars Geo'ge?" he asked in amazement.

"Yes, Plato. I 'm going to write a letter while I 'm in

town, and want you to take it. Meet me here in half an hour, and I 'll give you the letter. Meantime, keep your mouth shut."

"Yas, Mars Geo'ge," replied Plato with a grin that distended that organ unduly. That he did not keep it shut may be inferred from the fact that within the next half hour he had eaten and drunk fifty cents' worth of candy, ginger-pop, and other available delicacies that appealed to the youthful palate. Having nothing more to spend, and the high prices prevailing for some time after the war having left him capable of locomotion, Plato was promptly on hand at the appointed time and place.

Tryon placed a letter in Plato's hand, still sticky with molasses candy,—he had inclosed it in a second cover by way of protection. "Give that letter," he said, "to your teacher; don't say a word about it to a living soul; bring me an answer, and give it into my own hand, and you shall have another half dollar."

Tryon was quite aware that by a surreptitious correspondence he ran some risk of compromising Rena. But he had felt, as soon as he had indulged his first opportunity to talk of her, an irresistible impulse to see her and speak to her again. He could scarcely call at her boarding-place,—what possible proper excuse could a young white man have for visiting a colored woman? At the schoolhouse she would be surrounded by her pupils, and a private interview would be as difficult, with more eyes to remark and more tongues to comment upon it. He might address her by mail, but did not know how often she sent to the nearest post-office. A letter mailed in the town must pass through the hands of a postmaster notoriously inquisitive and evil-minded, who was familiar with

Tryon's handwriting and had ample time to attend to other people's business. To meet the teacher alone on the road seemed scarcely feasible, according to Plato's statement. A messenger, then, was not only the least of several evils, but really the only practicable way to communicate with Rena. He thought he could trust Plato, though miserably aware that he could not trust himself where this girl was concerned.

The letter handed by Tryon to Plato, and by the latter delivered with due secrecy and precaution, ran as follows:—

DEAR MISS WARWICK,—You may think it strange that I should address you after what has passed between us; but learning from my mother of your presence in the neighborhood, I am constrained to believe that you do not find my proximity embarrassing, and I cannot resist the wish to meet you at least once more, and talk over the circumstances of our former friendship. From a practical point of view this may seem superfluous, as the matter has been definitely settled. I have no desire to find fault with you; on the contrary, I wish to set myself right with regard to my own actions, and to assure you of my good wishes. In other words, since we must part, I would rather we parted friends than enemies. If nature and society—or Fate, to put it another way—have decreed that we cannot live together, it is nevertheless possible that we may carry into the future a pleasant though somewhat sad memory of a past friendship. Will you not grant me one interview? I appreciate the difficulty of arranging it; I have found it almost as hard to communicate with you by letter. I will suit myself to your convenience and meet you at any time and place you may designate. Please answer by bearer, who I think is trustworthy, and believe me, whatever your answer may be,

Respectfully yours,

G. T.

The next day but one Tryon received through the mail the following reply to his letter:—

GEORGE TRYON, ESQ.

Dear Sir,—I have requested your messenger to say that I will answer your letter by mail, which I shall now proceed to do. I assure you that I was entirely ignorant of your residence in this neighborhood, or it would have been the last place on earth in which I should have set foot.

As to our past relations, they were ended by your own act. I frankly confess that I deceived you; I have paid the penalty, and have no complaint to make. I appreciate the delicacy which has made you respect my brother's secret, and thank you for it. I remember the whole affair with shame and humiliation, and would willingly forget it.

As to a future interview, I do not see what good it would do either of us. You are white, and you have given me to understand that I am black. I accept the classification, however unfair, and the consequences, however unjust, one of which is that we cannot meet in the same parlor, in the same church, at the same table, or anywhere, in social intercourse; upon a steamboat we would not sit at the same table; we could not walk together on the street, or meet publicly anywhere and converse, without unkind remark. As a white man, this might not mean a great deal to you; as a woman, shut out already by my color from much that is desirable, my good name remains my most valuable possession. I beg of you to let me alone. The best possible proof you can give me of your good wishes is to relinquish any desire or attempt to see me. I shall have finished my work here in a few days. I have other troubles, of which you know nothing, and any meeting with you would only add to a burden which is already as much as I can bear. To speak of parting is superfluous—we have already parted. It were idle to dream of a future friendship between people so widely different in station. Such a friendship, if possible in itself, would never be tolerated by the lady whom you are to marry, with whom you drove by my schoolhouse the other day. A gentleman so loyal to his race and its traditions as you have shown yourself could not be less faithful to the lady to whom he has lost his heart and his memory in three short months.

No, Mr. Tryon, our romance is ended, and better so. We could never have been happy. I have found a work in which I may be of service to others who have fewer opportunities than mine have been. Leave me in peace, I beseech you, and I shall soon pass out of your neighborhood as I have passed out of your life, and hope to pass out of your memory.

Yours very truly,
ROWENA WALDEN.

XXX
AN UNUSUAL HONOR

To Rena's high-strung and sensitive nature, already under very great tension from her past experience, the ordeal of the next few days was a severe one. On the one hand, Jeff Wain's infatuation had rapidly increased, in view of her speedy departure. From Mrs. Tryon's remark about Wain's wife Amanda, and from things Rena had since learned, she had every reason to believe that this wife was living, and that Wain must be aware of the fact. In the light of this knowledge, Wain's former conduct took on a blacker significance than, upon reflection, she had charitably clothed it with after the first flush of indignation. That he had not given up his design to make love to her was quite apparent, and, with Amanda alive, his attentions, always offensive since she had gathered their import, became in her eyes the expression of a villainous purpose, of which she could not speak to others, and from which she felt safe only so long as she took proper precautions against it. In a week her school would be over, and then she would get Elder Johnson, or some one else than Wain, to take her back to Patesville. True, she might abandon her school and go at once; but her work would be incomplete, she would have violated her contract, she would lose her salary for the month, explanations would be necessary, and would not be forthcoming, She might feign sickness,—indeed, it would scarcely be feigning, for she felt far from well; she had never, since her illness, quite recovered her former vigor—but the inconvenience to others would be the same, and her self-sacrifice would have had, at its very first trial, a lame and impotent conclusion. She had as yet no fear of personal violence from Wain; but, under the circumstances, his attentions were an insult. He was evidently bent upon conquest, and vain enough to think he might achieve it by virtue of his personal attractions. If he could have understood how she loathed the sight of his narrow eyes, with their puffy lids, his thick, tobacco-stained lips, his doubtful teeth, and his unwieldy person, Wain, a monument of conceit that he was, might have shrunk, even in his own estimation, to something like his real proportions. Rena believed that, to defend herself from persecution at his hands, it was only necessary that she never let him find her alone. This, however, required constant watchfulness. Relying upon his own powers, and upon a woman's weakness and aversion to scandal, from which not even the purest may always escape unscathed, and convinced by her former silence that he had nothing serious to fear, Wain made it a point to be present at every public place where she might be. He assumed, in conversation with her which she could not avoid, and stated to others, that she had left his house because of a previous promise to divide the time of her stay between Elder Johnson's house and his own. He volunteered to teach a class in the Sunday-school which Rena conducted at the colored Methodist church, and when she remained to service, occupied a seat conspicuously near her own. In addition to these public demonstrations, which it was impossible to escape, or, it seemed, with so thick-skinned an individual as Wain, even to discourage, she was secretly and uncomfortably conscious that she could scarcely stir abroad without the risk of encountering one of two men, each of whom was on the lookout for an opportunity to find her alone.

The knowledge of Tryon's presence in the vicinity had been almost as much as Rena could bear. To it must be added the consciousness that he, too, was pursuing her, to what end she could not tell. After his letter to her brother, and the feeling therein displayed, she found it necessary to crush once or twice a wild hope that, her secret being still unknown save to a friendly few, he might return and claim her. Now, such an outcome would be impossible. He had become engaged to another woman,—this in itself would be enough to keep him from her, if it were not an index of a vastly more serious barrier, a proof that he had never loved her. If he had loved her truly, he would never have forgotten her in three short months,—three long months they had heretofore seemed to her, for in them she had lived a lifetime of experience. Another impassable barrier lay in the fact that his mother had met her, and that she was known in the neighborhood. Thus cut off from any hope that she might be anything to him, she had no wish to meet her former lover; no possible good could come of such a meeting; and yet her fluttering heart told her that if he should come, as his letter foreshadowed that he might,—if he should come, the loving George of old, with soft words and tender smiles and specious talk of friendship—ah! then, her heart would break! She must not meet him—at any cost she must avoid him.

But this heaping up of cares strained her endurance to the breaking-point. Toward the middle of the last week, she knew that she had almost reached the limit, and was haunted by a fear that she might break down before the week was over. Now her really fine nature rose to the emergency, though she mustered her forces with a great effort. If she could keep Wain at his distance and avoid Tryon for three days longer, her school labors would be ended and she might retire in peace and honor.

"Miss Rena," said Plato to her on Tuesday, "ain't it 'bout time I wuz gwine home wid you ag'in?"

"You may go with me to-morrow, Plato," answered the teacher.

After school Plato met an anxious-eyed young man in the woods a short distance from the school-house.

"Well, Plato, what news?"

"I 's gwine ter see her home ter-morrer, Mars Geo'ge."

"To-morrow!" replied Tryon; "how very unfortunate! I wanted you to go to town to-morrow to take an important message for me. I 'm sorry, Plato—you might have earned another dollar."

To lie is a disgraceful thing, and yet there are times when, to a lover's mind, love dwarfs all ordinary laws. Plato scratched his head disconsolately, but suddenly a bright thought struck him.

"Can't I go ter town fer you atter I 've seed her home, Mars Geo'ge?"

"N-o, I'm afraid it would be too late," returned Tryon doubtfully.

"Den I'll haf ter ax 'er ter lemme go nex' day," said Plato, with resignation. The honor might be postponed or, if necessary, foregone; the opportunity to earn a dollar was the chance of a lifetime and must not be allowed to slip.

"No, Plato," rejoined Tryon, shaking his head, "I should n't want to deprive you of so great a pleasure." Tryon was entirely sincere in this characterization of Plato's chance; he would have given many a dollar to be sure of Plato's place and Plato's welcome. Rena's letter had re-inflamed his smouldering passion; only opposition was needed to fan it to a white heat. Wherein lay the great superiority of his position, if he was denied the right to speak to the one person in the world whom he most cared to address? He felt some dim realization of the tyranny of caste, when he found it not merely pressing upon an inferior people who had no right to expect anything better, but barring his own way to something that he desired. He meant her no harm—but he must see her. He could never marry her now—but he must see her. He was conscious of a certain relief at the thought that he had not asked Blanche Leary to be his wife. His hand was unpledged. He could not marry the other girl, of course, but they must meet again. The rest he would leave to Fate, which seemed reluctant to disentangle threads which it had woven so closely.

"I think, Plato, that I see an easier way out of the difficulty. Your teacher, I imagine, merely wants some one to see her safely home. Don't you think, if you should go part of the way, that I might take your place for the rest, while you did my errand?"

"Why, sho'ly, Mars Geo'ge, you could take keer er her better 'n I could—better 'n anybody could—co'se you could!"

Mars Geo'ge was white and rich, and could do anything. Plato was proud of the fact that he had once belonged to Mars Geo'ge. He could not conceive of any one so powerful as Mars Geo'ge, unless it might be God, of whom Plato had heard more or less, and even here the comparison might not be quite fair to Mars Geo'ge, for Mars Geo'ge was the younger of the two. It would un-

217

doubtedly be a great honor for the teacher to be escorted home by Mars Geo'ge. The teacher was a great woman, no doubt, and looked white; but Mars Geo'ge was the real article. Mars Geo'ge had never been known to go with a black woman before, and the teacher would doubtless thank Plato for arranging that so great an honor should fall upon her. Mars Ge'oge had given him fifty cents twice, and would now give him a dollar. Noble Mars Geo'ge! Fortunate teacher! Happy Plato!

"Very well, Plato. I think we can arrange it so that you can kill the two rabbits at one shot. Suppose that we go over the road that she will take to go home."

They soon arrived at the schoolhouse. School had been out an hour, and the clearing was deserted. Plato led the way by the road through the woods to a point where, amid somewhat thick underbrush, another path intersected the road they were following.

"Now, Plato," said Tryon, pausing here, "this would be a good spot for you to leave the teacher and for me to take your place. This path leads to the main road, and will take you to town very quickly. I should n't say anything to the teacher about it at all; but when you and she get here, drop behind and run along this path until you meet me,—I 'll be waiting a few yards down the road,— and then run to town as fast as your legs will carry you. As soon as you are gone, I 'll come out and tell the teacher that I 've sent you away on an errand, and will myself take your place. You shall have a dollar, and I 'll ask her to let you go home with her the next day. But you must n't say a word about it, Plato, or you won't get the dollar, and I 'll not ask the teacher to let you go home with her again."

"All right, Mars Geo'ge, I ain't gwine ter say no mo' d'n ef de cat had my tongue."

XXXI
IN DEEP WATERS

RENA was unusually fatigued at the close of her school on Wednesday afternoon. She had been troubled all day with a headache, which, beginning with a dull pain, had gradually increased in intensity until every nerve was throbbing like a trip-hammer. The pupils seemed unusually stupid. A discouraging sense of the insignificance of any part she could perform towards the education of three million people with a school term of two months a year hung over her spirit like a pall. As the object of Wain's attentions, she had begun to feel somewhat like a wild creature who hears the pursuers on its track, and has the fear of capture added to the fatigue of flight. But when this excitement had gone too far and had neared the limit of exhaustion came Tryon's letter, with the resulting surprise and consternation. Rena had keyed herself up to a heroic pitch to answer it; but when the inevitable reaction came, she was overwhelmed with a sickening sense of her own weakness. The things which in another sphere had constituted her strength and shield were now her undoing, and exposed her to dangers from which they lent her no protection. Not only was this her position in theory, but the pursuers were already at her heels. As the day wore on, these dark thoughts took on an added gloom, until, when the hour to dismiss school arrived, she felt as though she had not a friend in the world. This feeling was accentuated by a letter which she had that morning received from her mother, in which Mis' Molly spoke very highly of Wain, and plainly expressed the hope that her daughter might like him so well that she would prefer to remain in Sampson County.

Plato, bright-eyed and alert, was waiting in the school-yard until the teacher should be ready to start. Having warned away several smaller children who had hung a-round after school as though to share his prerogative of accompanying the teacher, Plato had swung himself into the low branches of an oak at the edge of the clearing, from which he was hanging by his legs, head downward. He dropped from this reposeful attitude when the teacher appeared at the door, and took his place at her side.

A premonition of impending trouble caused the teacher to hesitate. She wished that she had kept more of the pupils behind. Something whispered that danger lurked in the road she customarily followed. Plato seemed insignificantly small and weak, and she felt miserably unable to cope with any difficult or untoward situation.

"Plato," she suggested, "I think we 'll go round the other way to-night, if you don't mind."

Visions of Mars Geo'ge disappointed, of a dollar unearned and unspent, flitted through the narrow brain which some one, with the irony of ignorance or of knowledge, had mocked with the name of a great philosopher. Plato was not an untruthful lad, but he seldom had the opportunity to earn a dollar. His imagination, spurred on by the instinct of self-interest, rose to the emergency.

"I 's feared you mought git snake-bit gwine roun' dat way, Miss Rena. My brer Jim kill't a water-moccasin down dere yistiddy 'bout ten feet long."

Rena had a horror of snakes, with which the swamp by which the other road ran was infested. Snakes were a vivid reality; her presentiment was probably a mere depression of spirits due to her condition of nervous exhaustion. A cloud had come up and threatened rain, and the wind was rising ominously. The old way was the shorter; she wanted above all things to get to Elder Johnson's and go to bed. Perhaps sleep would rest her tired brain—she could not imagine herself feeling worse, unless she should break down altogether.

She plunged into the path and hastened forward so as to reach home before the approaching storm. So completely was she absorbed in her own thoughts that she scarcely noticed that Plato himself seemed preoccupied. Instead of capering along like a playful kitten or puppy, he walked by her side unusually silent. When they had gone a short distance and were approaching a path which intersected their road at something near a right angle, the teacher missed Plato. He had dropped behind a moment before; now he had disappeared entirely. Her vague alarm of a few moments before returned with redoubled force.

"Plato!" she called; "Plato!"

There was no response, save the soughing of the wind through the swaying treetops. She stepped hastily forward, wondering if this were some childish prank. If so, it was badly timed, and she would let Plato feel the weight of her displeasure.

Her forward step had brought her to the junction of

the two paths, where she paused doubtfully. The route she had been following was the most direct way home, but led for quite a distance through the forest, which she did not care to traverse alone. The intersecting path would soon take her to the main road, where she might find shelter or company, or both. Glancing around again in search of her missing escort, she became aware that a man was approaching her from each of the two paths. In one she recognized the eager and excited face of George Tryon, flushed with anticipation of their meeting, and yet grave with uncertainty of his reception. Advancing confidently along the other path she saw the face of Jeff Wain, drawn, as she imagined in her anguish, with evil passions which would stop at nothing.

What should she do? There was no sign of Plato—for aught she could see or hear of him, the earth might have swallowed him up. Some deadly serpent might have stung him. Some wandering rabbit might have tempted him aside. Another thought struck her. Plato had been very quiet—there had been something on his conscience—perhaps he had betrayed her! But to which of the two men, and to what end?

The problem was too much for her overwrought brain. She turned and fled. A wiser instinct might have led her forward. In the two conflicting dangers she might have found safety. The road after all was a public way. Any number of persons might meet there accidentally. But she saw only the darker side of the situation. To turn to Tryon for protection before Wain had by some overt act manifested the evil purpose which she as yet only suspected would be, she imagined, to acknowledge a previous secret acquaintance with Tryon, thus placing her reputation at Wain's mercy, and to charge herself with a burden of obligation toward a man whom she wished to avoid and had refused to meet. If, on the other hand, she should go forward to meet Wain, he would undoubtedly offer to accompany her homeward. Tryon would inevitably observe the meeting, and suppose it prearranged. Not for the world would she have him think so—why she should care for his opinion, she did not stop to argue. She turned and fled, and to avoid possible pursuit, struck into the underbrush at an angle which she calculated would bring her in a few rods to another path which would lead quickly into the main road. She had run only a few yards when she found herself in the midst of a clump of prickly shrubs and briars. Meantime the storm had burst; the rain fell in torrents. Extricating herself from the thorns, she pressed forward, but instead of coming out upon the road, found herself penetrating deeper and deeper into the forest.

The storm increased in violence. The air grew darker and darker. It was near evening, the clouds were dense, the thick woods increased the gloom. Suddenly a blinding flash of lightning pierced the darkness, followed by a sharp clap of thunder. There was a crash of falling timber. Terror-stricken, Rena flew forward through the forest, the underbrush growing closer and closer as she advanced. Suddenly the earth gave way beneath her feet and she sank into a concealed morass. By clasping the trunk of a neighboring sapling she extricated herself with an effort, and realized with a horrible certainty that she was lost in the swamp.

Turning, she tried to retrace her steps. A flash of lightning penetrated the gloom around her, and barring her path she saw a huge black snake,—harmless enough, in fact, but to her excited imagination frightful in appearance. With a wild shriek she turned again, staggered forward a few yards, stumbled over a projecting root, and fell heavily to the earth.

When Rena had disappeared in the underbrush, Tryon and Wain had each instinctively set out in pursuit of her, but owing to the gathering darkness, the noise of the storm, and the thickness of the underbrush, they missed not only Rena but each other, and neither was aware of the other's presence in the forest. Wain kept up the chase until the rain drove him to shelter. Tryon, after a few minutes, realized that she had fled to escape him, and that to pursue her would be to defeat rather than promote his purpose. He desisted, therefore, and returning to the main road, stationed himself at a point where he could watch Elder Johnson's house, and having waited for a while without any signs of Rena, concluded that she had taken refuge in some friendly cabin. Turning homeward disconsolately as night came on, he intercepted Plato on his way back from town, and pledged him to inviolable secrecy so effectually that Plato, when subsequently questioned, merely answered that he had stopped a moment to gather some chinquapins, and when he had looked around the teacher was gone.

Rena not appearing at supper-time nor for an hour later, the elder, somewhat anxious, made inquiries about the neighborhood, and finding his guest at no place where she might be expected to stop, became somewhat alarmed. Wain's house was the last to which he went. He had surmised that there was some mystery connected with her leaving Wain's, but had never been given any definite information about the matter. In response to his inquiries, Wain expressed surprise, but betrayed a certain self-consciousness which did not escape the elder's eye. Returning home, he organized a search-party from his own family and several near neighbors, and set out with dogs and torches to scour the woods for the missing teacher. A couple of hours later, they found her lying unconscious in the edge of the swamp, only a few rods from a well-defined path which would soon have led her to the open highway. Strong arms lifted her gently and bore her home. Mrs. Johnson undressed her and put her to bed, administering a homely remedy, of which whiskey was the principal ingredient, to counteract the effects of the exposure. There was a doctor within five miles, but no one thought of sending for him, nor was it at all likely that it would have been possible to get him for such a case at such an hour.

Rena's illness, however, was more deeply seated than her friends could imagine. A tired body, in sympathy with an overwrought brain, had left her peculiarly susceptible to the nervous shock of her forest experience. The exposure for several hours in her wet clothing to the damps and miasma of the swamp had brought on an attack of brain fever. The next morning, she was delirious. One of the children took word to the schoolhouse that the teacher was sick and there would be no school that day. A number of curious and sympathetic people came in from time to time and suggested various remedies, several of which old Mrs. Johnson, with catholic impartiality, administered to the helpless teacher, who from delirium gradually sunk into a heavy stupor scarcely distinguishable from sleep. It was predicted that she would probably be well in the morning; if not, it would then be time to consider seriously the question of sending for a doctor.

XXXII
THE POWER OF LOVE

AFTER Tryon's failure to obtain an interview with Rena through Plato's connivance, he decided upon a different course of procedure. In a few days her school term would be finished. He was not less desirous to see her, was indeed as much more eager as opposition would be likely to make a very young man who was accustomed to having his own way, and whose heart, as he had discovered, was more deeply and permanently involved than he had imagined. His present plan was to wait until the end of the school; then, when Rena went to Clinton on the Saturday or Monday to draw her salary for the month, he would see her in the town, or, if necessary, would follow her to Patesville. No power on earth should keep him from her long, but he had no desire to interfere in any way with the duty which she owed to others. When the school was over and her work completed, then he would have his innings. Writing letters was too unsatisfactory a method of communication—he must see her face to face.

The first of his three days of waiting had passed, when, about ten o'clock on the morning of the second day, which seemed very long in prospect, while driving along the road toward Clinton, he met Plato, with a rabbit trap in his hand.

"Well, Plato," he asked, "why are you absent from the classic shades of the academy to-day?"

"Hoddy, Mars Geo'ge. W'at wuz dat you say?"

"Why are you not at school to-day?"

"Ain' got no teacher, Mars Geo'ge. Teacher 's gone!"

"Gone!" exclaimed Tryon, with a sudden leap of the heart. "Gone where? What do you mean?"

"Teacher got los' in de swamp, night befo' las', 'cause Plato wa'n't dere ter show her de way out'n de woods. Elder Johnson foun' 'er wid dawgs and tawches, an' fotch her home an' put her ter bed. No school yistiddy. She wuz out'n her haid las' night, an' dis mawnin' she wuz gone."

Gone where?"

"Dey don' nobody know whar, suh."

Leaving Plato abruptly, Tryon hastened down the road toward Elder Johnson's cabin. This was no time to stand on punctilio. The girl had been lost in the woods in the storm, amid the thunder and lightning and the pouring rain. She was sick with fright and exposure, and he was the cause of it all. Bribery, corruption, and falsehood had brought punishment in their train, and the innocent had suffered while the guilty escaped. He must learn at once what had become of her. Reaching Elder Johnson's house, he drew up by the front fence and gave the customary halloa, which summoned a woman to the door.

"Good-morning," he said, nodding unconsciously, with the careless politeness of a gentleman to his inferiors. "I 'm Mr. Tryon. I have come to inquire about the sick teacher."

"Why, suh," the woman replied respectfully, "she got los' in de woods night befo' las', an' she wuz out'n her min' most er de time yistiddy. Las' night she must 'a' got out er bed an' run away w'en eve'ybody wuz soun' asleep, fer dis mawnin' she wuz gone, an' none er us knows whar she is."

"Has any search been made for her?"

"Yas, suh, my husban' an' de child'en has been huntin' roun' all de mawnin', an' he's gone ter borry a hoss now ter go fu'ther. But Lawd knows dey ain' no tellin' whar she 'd go, 'less'n she got her min' back sence she lef'."

Tryon's mare was in good condition. He had money in his pocket and nothing to interfere with his movements. He set out immediately on the road to Patesville, keeping a lookout by the roadside, and stopping each person he met to inquire if a young woman, apparently ill, had been seen traveling along the road on foot. No one had met such a traveler. When he had gone two or three miles, he drove through a shallow branch that crossed the road. The splashing of his horse's hoofs in the water prevented him from hearing a low groan that came from the woods by the roadside.

He drove on, making inquiries at each farm-house and of every person whom he encountered. Shortly after crossing the branch, he met a young negro with a cartload of tubs and buckets and piggins, and asked him if he had seen on the road a young white woman with dark eyes and hair, apparently sick or demented. The young man answered in the negative, and Tryon pushed forward anxiously.

At noon he stopped at a farmhouse and swallowed a hasty meal. His inquiries here elicited no information, and he was just leaving when a young man came in late to dinner and stated, in response to the usual question, that he had met, some two hours before, a young woman who answered Tryon's description, on the Lillington road, which crossed the main road to Patesville a short distance beyond the farmhouse. He had spoken to the woman. At first she had paid no heed to his question. When addressed a second time, she had answered in a rambling and disconnected way, which indicated to his mind that there was something wrong with her.

Tryon thanked his informant and hastened to the Lillington road. Stopping as before to inquire, he followed the woman for several hours, each mile of the distance taking him farther away from Patesville. From time to time he heard of the woman. Toward nightfall he found her. She was white enough, with the sallowness of the sandhill poor white. She was still young, perhaps, but poverty and a hard life made her look older than she ought. She was not fair, and she was not Rena. When Tryon came up to her, she was sitting on the doorsill of a miserable cabin, and held in her hand a bottle, the contents of which had never paid any revenue tax. She had walked twenty miles that day, and had beguiled the tedium of the journey by occasional potations, which probably accounted for the incoherency of speech which several of those who met her had observed. When Tryon drew near, she tendered him the bottle with tipsy cordiality. He turned in disgust and retraced his steps to the Patesville road, which he did not reach until nightfall. As it was too dark to prosecute the search with any chance of success, he secured lodging for the night, intending to resume his quest early in the morning.

XXXIII
A MULE AND A CART

FRANK FOWLER'S heart was filled with longing for a sight of Rena's face. When she had gone away first, on the ill-fated trip to South Carolina, her absence had left an aching void in his life; he had missed her cheerful smile, her pleasant words, her graceful figure moving about across the narrow street. His work had grown monotonous during her absence; the clatter of hammer and mallet, that had seemed so merry when punctuated now and then by the strains of her voice, became a mere humdrum rapping of wood upon wood and iron upon iron. He had sought work in South Carolina with the hope that he might see her. He had satisfied this hope, and had tried in vain to do her a service; but Fate had been against her; her castle of cards had come tumbling down. He felt that her sorrow had brought her nearer to him. The distance between them depended very much upon their way of looking at things. He knew that her experience had dragged her through the valley of humiliation. His unselfish devotion had reacted to refine and elevate his own spirit. When he heard the suggestion, after her second departure, that she might marry Wain, he could not but compare himself with this new aspirant. He, Frank, was a man, an honest man—a better man than the shifty scoundrel with whom she had ridden away. She was but a woman, the best and sweetest and loveliest of all women, but yet a woman. After a few short years of happiness or sorrow,—little of joy, perhaps, and much of sadness, which had begun already,—they would both be food for worms. White people, with a deeper wisdom perhaps than they used in their own case, regarded Rena and himself as very much alike. They were certainly both made by the same God, in much the same physical and mental mould; they breathed the same air, ate the same food, spoke the same speech, loved and hated, laughed and cried, lived and would die, the same. If God had meant to rear any impassable barrier between people of contrasting complexions, why did He not express the prohibition as He had done between other orders of creation?

When Rena had departed for Sampson County, Frank had reconciled himself to her absence by the hope of her speedy return. He often stepped across the street to talk to Mis' Molly about her. Several letters had passed between mother and daughter, and in response to Frank's inquiries his neighbor uniformly stated that Rena was well and doing well, and sent her love to all inquiring friends. But Frank observed that Mis' Molly, when pressed as to the date of Rena's return, grew more and more indefinite; and finally the mother, in a burst of confidential friendship, told Frank of all her hopes with reference to the stranger from down the country.

"Yas, Frank," she concluded, "it 'll be her own fault ef she don't become a lady of proputty, fer Mr. Wain is rich, an' owns a big plantation, an' hires a lot of hands, and is a big man in the county. He 's crazy to git her, an' it all lays in her own han's."

Frank did not find this news reassuring. He believed that Wain was a liar and a scoundrel. He had nothing more than his intuitions upon which to found this belief, but it was none the less firm. If his estimate of the man's character were correct, then his wealth might be a fiction, pure and simple. If so, the truth should be known to Mis' Molly, so that instead of encouraging a marriage with Wain, she would see him in his true light, and interpose to rescue her daughter from his importunities. A day or two after this conversation, Frank met in the town a negro from Sampson County, made his acquaintance, and inquired if he knew a man by the name of Jeff Wain.

"Oh, Jeff Wain!" returned the countryman slightingly; "yas, I knows 'im, an' don' know no good of 'im. One er dese yer biggity, braggin' niggers—talks lack he own de whole county, an' ain't wuth no mo' d'n I is—jes' a big bladder wid a handful er shot rattlin' roun' in it. Had a wife, when I wuz dere, an' beat her an' 'bused her so she had ter run away."

This was alarming information. Wain had passed in the town as a single man, and Frank had had no hint that he had ever been married. There was something wrong somewhere. Frank determined that he would find out the truth and, if possible, do something to protect Rena against the obviously evil designs of the man who had taken her away. The barrel factory had so affected the cooper's trade that Peter and Frank had turned their attention more or less to the manufacture of small woodenware for domestic use. Frank's mule was eating off its own head, as the saying goes. It required but little effort to persuade Peter that his son might take a load of buckets and tubs and piggins into the country and sell them or trade them for country produce at a profit.

In a few days Frank had his stock prepared, and set out on the road to Sampson County. He went about thirty miles the first day, and camped by the roadside for the night, resuming the journey at dawn. After driving for an hour through the tall pines that overhung the road like the stately arch of a cathedral aisle, weaving a carpet for the earth with their brown spines and cones, and soothing the ear with their ceaseless murmur, Frank stopped to water his mule at a point where the white, sandy road, widening as it went, sloped downward to a clear-running branch. On the right a bay-tree bending over the stream mingled the heavy odor of its flowers with the delicate perfume of a yellow jessamine vine that had overrun a clump of saplings on the left. From a neighboring tree a silver-throated mocking-bird poured out a flood of riotous melody. A group of minnows, startled by the splashing of the mule's feet, darted away into the shadow of the thicket, their quick passage leaving the amber water filled with laughing light.

The mule drank long and lazily, while over Frank stole thoughts in harmony with the peaceful scene,—thoughts of Rena, young and beautiful, her friendly smile, her pensive dark eyes. He would soon see her now, and if she had any cause for fear or unhappiness, he would place himself at her service—for a day, a week, a month, a year, a lifetime, if need be.

His reverie was broken by a slight noise from the thicket at his left. "I wonder who dat is?" he muttered. "It soun's mighty quare, ter say de leas'."

He listened intently for a moment, but heard nothing further. "It must 'a' be'n a rabbit er somethin' scamp'in' th'ough de woods. G'long dere, Cæsar!"

As the mule stepped forward, the sound was repeated. This time it was distinctly audible, the long, low moan of some one in sickness or distress.

"Dat ain't no rabbit," said Frank to himself. "Dere 's somethin' wrong dere. Stan' here, Cæsar, till I look inter dis matter."

Pulling out from the branch, Frank sprang from the saddle and pushed his way cautiously through the outer edge of the thicket.

"Good Lawd!" he exclaimed with a start, "it 's a woman—a w'ite woman!"

The slender form of a young woman lay stretched upon the ground in a small open space a few yards in extent. Her face was turned away, and Frank could see at first only a tangled mass of dark brown hair, matted with twigs and leaves and cockleburs, and hanging in wild profusion around her neck.

Frank stood for a moment irresolute, debating the serious question whether he should investigate further with a view to rendering assistance, or whether he should put as great a distance as possible between himself and this victim, as she might easily be, of some violent crime, lest he should himself be suspected of it—a not unlikely contingency, if he were found in the neighborhood and the woman should prove unable to describe her assailant. While he hesitated, the figure moved restlessly, and a voice murmured:—

"Mamma, oh, mamma!"

The voice thrilled Frank like an electric shock. Trembling in every limb, he sprang forward toward the prostrate figure. The woman turned her head, and he saw that it was Rena. Her gown was torn and dusty, and fringed with burs and briars. When she had wandered forth, half delirious, pursued by imaginary foes, she had not stopped to put on her shoes, and her little feet were blistered and swollen and bleeding. Frank knelt by her side and lifted her head on his arm. He put his hand upon her brow; it was burning with fever.

"Miss Rena! Rena! don't you know me?"

She turned her wild eyes on him suddenly. "Yes, I know you, Jeff Wain. Go away from me! Go away!"

Her voice rose to a scream; she struggled in his grasp and struck at him fiercely with her clenched fists. Her sleeve fell back and disclosed the white scar made by his own hand so many years before.

"You're a wicked man," she panted. "Don't touch me! I hate you and despise you!"

Frank could only surmise how she had come here, in such a condition. When she spoke of Wain in this manner, he drew his own conclusions. Some deadly villainy of Wain's had brought her to this pass. Anger stirred his nature to the depths, and found vent in curses on the author of Rena's misfortunes.

"Damn him!" he groaned. "I'll have his heart's blood fer dis, ter de las' drop!"

Rena now laughed and put up her arms appealingly. "George," she cried, in melting tones, "dear George, do you love me? How much do you love me? Ah, you don't love me!" she moaned; "I 'm black; you don't love me; you despise me!"

Her voice died away into a hopeless wail. Frank knelt by her side, his faithful heart breaking with pity, great tears rolling untouched down his dusky cheeks.

"Oh, my honey, my darlin'," he sobbed, "Frank loves you better 'n all de worl'."

Meantime the sun shone on as brightly as before, the mocking-bird sang yet more joyously. A gentle breeze sprang up and wafted the odor of bay and jessamine past them on its wings. The grand triumphal sweep of nature's onward march reeked nothing of life's little tragedies.

When the first burst of his grief was over, Frank brought water from the branch, bathed Rena's face and hands and feet, and forced a few drops between her reluctant lips. He then pitched the cartload of tubs, buckets, and piggins out into the road, and gathering dried leaves and pine-straw, spread them in the bottom of the cart. He stooped, lifted her frail form in his arms, and laid it on the leafy bed. Cutting a couple of hickory withes, he arched them over the cart, and gathering an armful of jessamine quickly wove it into an awning to protect her from the sun. She was quieter now, and seemed to fall asleep.

"Go ter sleep, honey," he murmured caressingly,—"go ter sleep, an' Frank 'll take you home ter yo' mammy!"

Toward noon he was met by a young white man, who peered inquisitively into the canopied cart.

"Hello!" exclaimed the stranger, "who 've you got there?"

"A sick woman, suh."

"Why, she 's white, as I'm a sinner!" he cried, after a closer inspection. "Look a-here, nigger, what are you doin' with this white woman?"

"She's not w'ite, boss,—she's a bright mulatter."

"Yas, mighty bright," continued the stranger suspiciously. "Where are you goin' with her?"

"I'm takin' her ter Patesville, ter her mammy."

The stranger passed on. Toward evening Frank heard hounds baying in the distance. A fox, weary with running, brush drooping, crossed the road ahead of the cart. Presently, the hounds straggled across the road, followed by two or three hunters on horseback, who stopped at sight of the strangely canopied cart. They stared at the sick girl and demanded who she was.

"I don't b'lieve she 's black at all," declared one, after Frank's brief explanation. "This nigger has a bad eye,— he 's up ter some sort of devilment. What ails the girl?"

"'Pears ter be some kind of a fever," replied Frank; adding diplomatically, "I don't know whether it 's ketchin' er no—she 's be'n out er her head most er de time."

They drew off a little at this. "I reckon it's all right," said the chief spokesman. The hounds were baying clamorously in the distance. The hunters followed the sound and disappeared in the woods.

Frank drove all day and all night, stopping only for brief periods of rest and refreshment. At dawn, from the top of the long white hill, he sighted the river bridge below. At sunrise he rapped at Mis' Molly's door.

Upon rising at dawn, Tryon's first step, after a hasty breakfast, was to turn back toward Clinton. He had wasted half a day in following the false scent on the Lillington road. It seemed, after reflection, unlikely that a woman seriously ill should have been able to walk any considerable distance before her strength gave out. In her delirium, too, she might have wandered in a wrong direction, imagining any road to lead to Patesville. It would be a good plan to drive back home, continuing his inquiries meantime, and ascertain whether or not she had been found by those who were seeking her, including many whom Tryon's inquiries had placed upon the alert. If she should prove still missing, he would resume the journey to Patesville and continue the search in that direction. She had probably not wandered far from the highroad; even in delirium she would be likely to avoid the deep woods, with which her illness was associated.

He had retraced more than half the distance to Clinton when he overtook a covered wagon. The driver, when questioned, said that he had met a young negro with a mule, and a cart in which lay a young woman, white to all appearance, but claimed by the negro to be a colored girl who had been taken sick on the road, and whom he was conveying home to her mother at Patesville. From a further description of the cart Tryon recognized it as the one he had met the day before. The woman could be no other than Rena. He turned his mare and set out swiftly on the road to Patesville.

If anything could have taken more complete possession of George Tryon at twenty-three than love successful and triumphant, it was love thwarted and denied. Never in the few brief delirious weeks of his courtship had he felt so strongly drawn to the beautiful sister of the popular lawyer, as he was now driven by an aching heart toward the same woman stripped of every adventitious advantage and placed, by custom, beyond the pale of marriage with men of his own race. Custom was tyranny. Love was the only law. Would God have made hearts to so yearn for one another if He had meant them to stay forever apart? If this girl should die, it would be he who had killed her, by his cruelty, no less surely than if with his own hand he had struck her down. He had been so dazzled by his own superiority, so blinded by his own glory, that he had ruthlessly spurned and spoiled the image of God in this fair creature, whom he might have had for his own treasure,—whom, please God, he would yet have, at any cost, to love and cherish while they both should live. There were difficulties—they had seemed insuperable, but love would surmount them. Sacrifices must be made, but if the world without love would be nothing, then why not give up the world for love? He would hasten to Patesville. He would find her; he would tell her that he loved her, that she was all the world to him, that he had come to marry her, and take her away where they might be happy together. He pictured to himself the joy that would light up her face; he felt her soft arms around his neck, her tremulous kisses upon his lips. If she were ill, his love would woo her back to health,— if disappointment and sorrow had contributed to her illness, joy and gladness should lead to her recovery.

He urged the mare forward; if she would but keep up her present pace, he would reach Patesville by nightfall.

Dr. Green had just gone down the garden path to his buggy at the gate. Mis' Molly came out to the back piazza, where Frank, weary and haggard, sat on the steps with Homer Pettifoot and Billy Oxendine, who, hearing of Rena's return, had come around after their day's work.

"Rena wants to see you, Frank," said Mis' Molly, with a sob.

He walked in softly, reverently, and stood by her bedside. She turned her gentle eyes upon him and put out her slender hand, which he took in his own broad palm.

"Frank," she murmured, "my good friend—my best friend—you loved me best of them all."

The tears rolled untouched down his cheeks. "I 'd 'a' died, fer you, Miss Rena," he said brokenly.

Mary B. threw open a window to make way for the passing spirit, and the red and golden glory of the setting sun, triumphantly ending his daily course, flooded the narrow room with light.

Between sunset and dark a traveler, seated in a dusty buggy drawn by a tired horse, crossed the long river bridge and drove up Front Street. Just as the buggy reached the gate in front of the house behind the cedars, a woman was tying a piece of crape upon the door-knob. Pale with apprehension, Tryon sat as if petrified, until a tall, side-whiskered mulatto came down the garden walk to the front gate.

"Who's dead?" demanded Tryon hoarsely, scarcely recognizing his own voice.

"A young cullud 'oman, suh," answered Homer Pettifoot, touching his hat, "Mis' Molly Walden's daughter Rena."